The *Miracle* of
TRISTAN RAY THOMPSON

ROBERT HERNANDEZ

ISBN 978-1-0980-5737-4 (paperback)
ISBN 978-1-0980-5738-1 (digital)

Copyright © 2020 by Robert Hernandez

All rights reserved. No part of this publication may be reproduced, distributed, or transmitted in any form or by any means, including photocopying, recording, or other electronic or mechanical methods without the prior written permission of the publisher. For permission requests, solicit the publisher via the address below.

Christian Faith Publishing, Inc.
832 Park Avenue
Meadville, PA 16335
www.christianfaithpublishing.com

Printed in the United States of America

THE MIRACLE OF TRISTAN RAY THOMPSON

My dear precious son Tristan,

There's so much I want to say to you. Just know, not a day goes by that I don't think of you. I miss your smile, your laugh, your voice, your humor, your brilliant intelligent mind, your love, and your compassion. I miss how you would always call me the day before and the day of my birthday and Mother's Day. It made those days, for me, so special. I just miss my precious son.

I want to tell you, Tris, that I'm sorry you suffered so much in your life. I suffered with you. I wanted to take all your pain away from you. On August 14, 2016, God ended your suffering. I used to pray for him to do that for you, but I didn't know it would involve you being taken from me and home to be with Jesus. That's the only comfort I get with your passing is knowing you no longer suffer and are living eternally with our Lord.

Tris, I want to share with you what my life with you was like. I loved being pregnant with you. To feel this little human being growing, living, and moving around in my stomach was such an awesome and beautiful experience. I remember when I gave birth to you and brought you home, all I wanted to do is hold you and love you forever. I was in awe of the miracle of you. I marveled at the beautiful creation and the masterpiece of our Heavenly Father that created you just for me as my son. I had asked him before you were conceived to bless me with a child, and you are who he chose for me.

You were such a happy baby boy, always smiling that beautiful smile of yours. And to hear you laugh, as babies laugh, brought such joy to my heart. What pleasure I had taking care of my precious baby boy. I couldn't get enough of you. How blessed I was being given the gift of you.

A funny memory that comes to my mind is when you were three years old, you came to me with excitement in your voice and said, "Mommy, come look! I found buried treasure in our backyard!" I went outside to see it, and what I saw was some of my "costume jewelry." (I never owned any valuable jewelry.) I played along like I was surprised but, of course, later had to tell you not to do it anymore.

Then came your toddler years. You were in constant motion, exploring the world around you. So inquisitive and smart. Talking by the age of two and knowing your ABCs. You loved me reading to you or teaching you new things. You were still a happy, carefree, pure, and innocent baby boy.

(That would change when you turned four years old. I would learn after your death that when we took a trip out West, you would be sexually violated by an adult male. You wrote on my computer how this event "tormented and haunted you in your life.") You grew through the "terrible twos, the tireless threes, and the fearless fours. But as I said, because of a traumatic event, you would change from the fearless four-year-old to a fearful four-year-old little boy.

Then you entered kindergarten, a shy little boy that didn't want to leave my side. You became an anxious, nervous little boy around this time. You had trouble being focused at school and was fidgety to the point your teacher thought you might have ADHD. It was suggested we take you to a doctor to find out if this was correct. And it was confirmed. You were put on medication, and it seemed to help some. When you were in the second grade, your teacher had a conference with me and said she'd heard some bad things about the medicine causing heart problems, and I immediately stopped giving it to you. You started struggling again in school and was getting in trouble for it. This went on for a number of years. I could tell it was affecting your self-esteem. I tried to encourage you, but deep down inside, I felt helpless as a parent.

One of many good memories of you that comes to my mind is the compassion you have shown even as a young boy. Many times, we've seen homeless people on the street, and you have asked me to give them something, which if I had it, I gave it. And then there was the day that I was busy cleaning the house, and I heard you crying. You were eleven years old at the time. I asked you what you were crying about. You said, "Mama, Trevor hardly has any toys. I've always had lots of toys. I feel so sorry for him." You loved your little baby brother so much. You just didn't know that when you were growing up as an only child that we had more money for things, and when Trevor was born, we didn't have as much money. It just melted my heart that you had so much love, care, and compassion for your baby brother.

This next memory is kind of sad but also showed your compassionate side. When your grandmother, whom you adored and she adored you, passed away in 1990, you became so depressed you had written out a will. You wanted your little brother to have everything that belonged to you. It was scary finding that letter that you'd written because when people write out a will, they either know they are going to die, or they want to die. Your dad and I made a decision, along with a doctor, to admit you into a hospital where you could get professional help. That was also where the doctor told us, "Your son has Tourette syndrome." I will never forget those words. Something strange started to happen to you right before you went into the hospital. You started with unusual movements to your body, grimacing in your face and speaking in a way that was not understood as language. In the year 1989, you would be diagnosed with Tourette syndrome. I remember looking up information in an old medical book that said this is "a bizarre psychiatric disorder." I thought, *Oh my god! My poor son! What challenges are we going to experience due to this illness?* I was afraid for you and for us. You were dealing with this Tourette syndrome and ADHD at the same time. It was very obvious how stressful and emotionally painful it was to you. It broke our hearts knowing you were dealing with so much for a young boy of your age and the fact that you were our precious, Tristan. The Tourette syndrome and the manifestations that happened with it would cause you so much anxiety and damage your self-esteem. It was then that I started seeing my son change from being somewhat happy to being an angry teenager.

Your dad and I took you for counseling, and you were once again put on medication. After a period of time, you said you hated the medicine and how it made you feel "drugged out." Even though it seemed like it was helping you, because you were spitting the pills out that we would find later, we made the decision to stop giving the medicine to you. Then, as before when you were younger, you started struggling again, and things would start to get much worse for you.

Eventually, over a few years, you went from not wanting to take prescribed medicine to taking unprescribed medicine and start drinking alcohol. I know you just wanted your pain to go away somehow. But the consequences of this decision led to even more traumatic suffering. You would spend most of the next twenty years suffering, even still in the madness of spending time in jails and prisons. I felt like I, too, was spending time there with you. I thought about so many things that could be taking place. I worried myself sick, thinking you were being harmed and you were suffering there. I worried it would cause you to go insane, especially because some of that time was spent in solitary confinement, in order to be protected from others. But it was there, in total isolation, that you grew even closer to God and would experience his peace that passes understanding. You would tell me about your studies of his word in the Bible. Wanting to know even more you requested many books over the years to read of Christian authors that studied and interpreted what they too had learned of his word.

During the times of you being released from your incarcerations, you would come out being more hopeful, happy, and positive. But the enemy, the devil or his demons, would swiftly come and lead you back into addiction, its madness, and create suffering for you that would continue to destroy that peace you had found in what you would call your "cave of meditation," being isolated from the world.

In 2013, you would go to prison for the last time in your life and stay there three years. On February 11, 2016, you came to Arizona to live with me and start a new life there. You said you didn't want to go back to Kentucky, where you knew everyone. You said you wanted a fresh start to start your new life over. I was so happy and excited for you. And finally, my son was with me again after being gone for way too long. I missed you so bad all those years over your lifetime you were away from me.

After being released, you did exceptionally well for a few months. But the emotional pain of your suffering life, and the demons that stalked you, would cause you to want once again want to be free from it all. It caused you to escape back into the dark world, the madness, and the suffering of addiction. Once again, the enemy would get you distracted and away from Jesus. As always, the torment you felt would be too much for you to bear.

It was the beginning of the last week of your life. Like the sad, scared boy that lived inside you, you would say like, I've heard multiple times in your short thirty-eight years, "Mama, I just want to be normal. I just want to be happy." You'd decided you wanted an end to your pain and torment. You wanted to go to a methadone clinic to get off drugs. During your short six-day treatment, you said it was the happiest you'd ever felt and that you had peace. On the sixth day of your treatment, they told you they would not be open on Sunday and would send you home with your medication.

We spent that Saturday at the Desert Museum in Tucson, Arizona, a place you fell in love with. Like a carefree young child, you took my friend and yours by the hand and joyfully led her around the museum, showing all the beauty of God's created desert with unique plant life and creatures.

On the way home from the museum, we were listening to the Christian radio station called K-Love. A song came on by Lincoln Brewster called "There Is Power." You rolled the window down and started singing as loud as you could out the window, like you wanted the whole world to hear this song about Jesus. Experiencing your joy with you about this gave me goose bumps, warmed my heart, gave me peace, and made me smile. And when the song was over, like a little child, you lay your head on my shoulder, as I was driving us home. What a beautiful memory for me, all that we experienced on your last day of living life.

The next morning, Sunday, August 14, 2016, I woke up and was going to take my dogs outside. Coming down the hallway, out of the corner of my eye, I saw you lying face down on the floor. My heart seemed to stop and felt like it had broken into a million pieces. I knew you were gone forever. My precious son, whom I had loved, whom I had suffered along with him during his pain and torment here on earth, was taken out of his suffering and home to be in heaven with Jesus.

These last three years have been almost too much to bear, losing the precious gift of you, my son, Tristan. Recently I recalled a memory of what you had told me many years ago. It was when I was living alone in Arizona. I was so sad, so lonely for you and the rest of my family. You called me from prison. I said, "Tris, I don't think I'm going to make it." Literally, I felt like I was dying slowly day by day.

You said, "Mama, please don't say that. I need you to be strong for me, for Trevor and Trey."

I stopped crying and got myself composed and said, "Okay, honey. I will. I will stay strong for you guys."

As painful as losing you has been for me, Tris, the comfort I get is knowing you no longer suffer, and you have the peace you so desperately needed and wanted. I now think of my precious Tristan, carefree as the child he was, once upon a time, running in a field of beautiful brilliantly colored flowers you told of many years ago. Till I see you again…

Love,
Mama

Tristan Thompson
February 5, 2015

Like Drops of Rain in the Ocean...

Like drops of rain in the ocean...of which, one could easily be driven mad at the burdensome task of attempting to retrace, drop by drop, every last drop of rain to get an accurate measurement of just how many drops were contained therein...so are the errors and regrets of my life... And like the ocean, in their collective massive totality, they sway back and forth, back and forth, with a hypnotizing momentum, a heavy accumulating dynamic, which, over and over, ends again and again in the rolling waves of guilt and remorse upon the worn shores of my conscience...the shores, they are empty of normal company; no drunken sunburnt college kids, no sand castles, no volley ball champs...just a pair of feet. One pair of feet upon which wave after wave crashes and yet goes no further than the toes.

Again, I could easily be driven mad at the surmising of the number of total drops that formed this, my ocean of emotions...but when I drift ashore time to time, I instead get caught up and lost in the mystery of grace as I behold the feet of the master...then drifting slowly back out to ocean.

My name is Tristan Ray Thompson. Yes, I may be this or that, Yes, I did this and that, or said this or that, or said this but meant that, but you know what...that is exactly why we are alike, my friend. None righteous—no, not one—for all have sinned and fallen short. If I have wronged you in any way, I wish I could take it back. I would have rather righted you. Come now, let's be reasonable; don't you think I would much rather have made you proud, or brought you joy? Helped instead of hurting? This ocean that I'm stranded in is of my own creation, comprised entirely of my mistakes.

While I can't give an accurate count of them all, I do give a sincere apology. While I can't undo it...I can try to mend and help now...show me how, show me where it hurts because, by nature, I am a healer. But most of all, know this...if you know me mostly by the bad things I've done, know that they too are as mere drops in an ocean of goodness that you've yet to behold in me...and with the help of the being whose nail-scarred feet I beheld upon the shores of my conscience...I will get a chance to show you better...that I seek to heal not harm, please forgive me. Peace to you. "TT"

This work was written to express the preciousness of the child, Tristan Ray Thompson. I had the privilege to come to know this child in a very unique way. It wasn't until after he went home to be with the Lord Jesus Christ that I encountered his many writings and poems, along with his comic videos.

It was amazing to me the amount of talent that this child possessed. So it is my privilege to share his story with you, the readers. He was a very compassionate person, especially where those that were considered unworthy by most of society. He himself was also considered unworthy by society, and this was a part of his lifelong struggle to be accepted by others. He endured a major tragedy when he was a young child of four years old. And this tragedy haunted him from that time forward. How he was able to endure can only be attributed to the grace and love of God that was in his life, even when he himself was unaware of it. I hope his writings will bring some sort of joy, just as they did me.

Tristan was a very intelligent young man, and I'm sure his writings will bear this truth out. This book is especially for those in life who may have experienced the same rejection from others that this child experienced, yet find hope that there can be peace. For I believe Tristan found this peace before he went home to be with the Lord Jesus Christ. And my prayer is that those of you who are looking for this same peace may also find it. His journey was filled with both ups and downs, but through it all, he remained a loving and caring child. I use the word *child* in describing this young man quite a bit, and the reason for this is the following, he was a child. Even at the age of thirty-eight, he remained just like a child. And the Word of God says, that in order for anyone to enter the Kingdom of heaven, they must become as a little child.

He had a great understanding concerning the truth of God's word. Yet because of his weakness of the flesh, he would allow himself to become overcome by his tragedies that he endured throughout his life. At those times, he would become once again lost to the truth of God's promises and wander into the craziness of this world. But as I've said before, I believe that in the end, he came back to the truth of God's promises, and there, he found the peace and acceptance he was always looking for.

ROBERT HERNANDEZ

May his story inspire you, the readers, and give you hope that God can work things out for our good if you allow his love to become a part of your life. With love for what this child allowed me to share, I give you Tristan Ray Thompson.

THE WORLD'S BEST UNKNOWN POET, WHOM THE WORLD NEVER KNEW

I have a story that I desire to share with the world. It's about a talented and gifted young man I had the privilege and honor of knowing. What was so unique about this young man was his compassion about those that have been less fortunate and rejected in life, for he himself had been rejected by most people in his life and by those of his own family. Yet through it all, he maintained a love and compassion for those that rejected him. What was so precious about this precious life was his ability to touch the lives and hearts of those he touched with an instant ability to express his great love for them, and they could feel his love.

He had a heart of compassion for those in this world who struggled, the less fortunate, the homeless, the rejected, those who felt the pain of not being accepted. When I say those that struggled and were less fortunate, I'm referring to the homeless, the abused, those that society has, for the most part, rejected as having little or no value. I believe the reason for this is the following—he himself was rejected by most in society as an outcast. I myself have been considered an outcast of society, so this is the reason this precious and gifted child, Tristan, and I met. Both considered outcasts by society in general.

To understand just how awesome this gifted young man was, I'd like to share the following information with those in the world, who will never have the opportunity to know this incredible precious child in person. This young man's name is Tristan Ray Thompson, and he was born in the great state of Kentucky. Even though I feel that I am less than adequate to convey Tristan's story in a worthy manner that it should be told, I intend to do my very best for this precious child. I go forward with the hope and prayer that the words I write can and will express how truly awesome and gifted and loved this precious young man truly was.

I started this story off by saying this child was the world's best unknown comic the world never knew! I was privileged to come to know this truth after he went home to be with the Lord, to view some videos he had made during the last six months of his life. He had such a unique style of presentation, I myself have never encountered writing such as his style presented. It was unique in his very own individualism, and in this manner, he presented it to the world.

I've also shared that this precious child was the best unknown poet the world never had the opportunity to know. I myself, at the time of this writing, had never read any of his material or anything this gifted child had ever written. So in order for you, the reader, to understand how I could write these words about Tristan, I would like to share with you from where I got this information from.

The following words were written on my computer by Tristan himself. He states the following, "Absolutely serious now… My life has been crazy, beyond crazy! Crazy really isn't the word that best describes my life. I believe that there is no lexicon or fringe vernacular to describe it! Total super high ups and super low downs. Man, so down…in the earth, but yet, *alive*, YET IN SOME KIND OF LITERAL DUNGEON OF DOOM! Under places…tunnels—holy crap, the tunnels, haunted, literally and full of wretched creatures, and people. But where does one go when you are a stranger in a strange land? An abject outcast! Exiled in the literal sense. My name is Tristan Ray Thompson…and I am many things, but there is one thing you need to understand, my readers, is that I am the best unknown poet this world never knew. I have the ability to show forth skills, and fringe vernaculars, grand eloquence, and super designed metaphors. But know this…I was here…I lived… And live still…AND HOW SAD IN THE END…Should I continue to deviate? Will they know that I am what I consider the best unknown poet the world has never known? Will something happen to this work of mine? I pray that something will, but today is July 14, 2016, and I am alive and in good hands. Amen."

This is what Tristan wrote about himself, and he believed it was for him as well, "As I was with Moses…so shall I be with you [spoken to Joshua…by Yahweh]. Also, spoken to me, for the Lord is not a respecter of persons, what He has done for Joshua, He shall also do for me."

So as you can see, this was my reason and purpose for not only writing this story about Tristan but also for the title of this writing. Since I began writing this story, I've spoken with Tristan's mom, Angie, and she has shared with me most of Tristan's writings. As I continue to write this story about Tristan, I'd like to share with you the reader just a small sample of what I consider to be the genius of Tristan.

INTO THE MIRACLES!

Tristan Ray Thompson
Written on April 30, 2013!

The step that is seldom taken,
Revealed in an ancient book,
Into the mystery.
Spellbinding symphony,
Where Joseph gained a ring.
And Paul did silence kings,
And water became wine,
And angels did merry fly.
And dead were raised amazed,
And empty was the grave,
This is the step,
That take's one's breath,
When miracles manifest.

I'd like to share with you the reader what I consider the interpretation of what I believe Tristan was trying to convey to you his readers, through this his poem. For Tristan's thoughts have been lost to this world due to his passing, but I hope and pray that through my presentation of his writings, I may convey to the world this gifted and talented young man's awesome heart.

I, for one, would have enjoyed hearing his own interpretation of his works, but sadly, I can only convey what I believe would be his interpretation of his works. This precious child had a wisdom that was truly unique. My own understanding of the above poem is as follows—"The step that is seldom taken…" For the most part, mankind has chosen to reject the belief in an all-powerful and all-knowing God—a being that is all present at all times, a being that is self-sufficient. So mankind refuses to travel this step that is seldom taken. He refuses to attempt to take this journey that would lead him or her to know and understand this being called the One true God.

But at the same time, there are those that have chosen to take the step that is seldom taken. And I believe Tristan was one of those that took this very step. For as you'll see in some later writings by Tristan, he wrote some very interesting things concerning the Lord God, Most High.

"Revealed in an ancient book..." I believe this is in reference to the Holy Bible. This declares that in times past, mankind has been led to write about certain wisdom that has been revealed to the world, along with certain knowledge and understanding. But from the many ancient books that man has written, there is only one book mankind was to acquire wisdom, knowledge, and understanding, and that book is the Holy Word of God. This I believe to be the real purpose by which mankind is to live his life upon this earth.

The all-powerful God has chosen to reveal all this wisdom, knowledge, and understanding to mankind so mankind could live the life God has purposed for men to live. And God has inspired certain men to write this revelation down. I for one would have enjoyed listening to Tristan expound upon these words that he wrote, but that privilege is no longer available to myself or the world. So I will do my best to try to give to you, the reader, what I believe would be his interpretation.

Revealed in an ancient book...

This declares to me that throughout the history of mankind, men were led to write about certain wisdom, knowledge, and understanding. They gathered this from various places and experiences. This they did using their own experiences and looking in various places, but from the many different places in which they looked for this wisdom, knowledge, and understanding, they were looking in the wrong places. There is only one book that contains the wisdom, knowledge, and understanding the world needs, and I believe that book is the Holy Bible of the one true God.

This is what God has purposed for mankind, and I believe the Word of God teaches us this in the book of Proverbs, chapter 1, verses 2 through 7. So let us hear what the Word of God has to say. "To know wisdom and instruction, The instruction of wisdom, Justice, judgment, and equity; To give prudence to the simple, To the young man knowledge and discretion… A wise man will hear and increase learning, And a man of understanding will attain wise counsel, To understand a proverb and an enigma, The words of the wise, and their riddles. The fear of the Lord is the beginning of knowledge, But fools despise wisdom and instruction." So let us go on to interpret the following words from Tristan's poem.

"Into the mystery…" Into the mystery, a journey was begun; a direction taken; a quest for wisdom, knowledge, and understanding. For myself, I believe this is the mystery that Tristan spoke of. Yet these very words were spoken by the one true God—this being that spoke all things into existence, the all-powerful God, as was written in the Holy Bible. When we as humans receive these words into our hearts, and as we walk them out in our lives, we will understand the mystery of coming to know this all-powerful being known as God.

And we can come to know His wisdom, knowledge, and understanding, and His mystery, which has been revealed in His Holy Word, so we as mankind could learn to live life as He intended. The mystery has been hidden from before the ages and generations. This has now been revealed to all of mankind, if a man chooses to receive it. But this mystery has now been revealed, and if those that receive this wisdom, knowledge, and understanding from the Lord God, and used it as God has purposed, we shall understand the mystery, for God has willed to make known unto all those that choose to receive His Word what are the riches of the glory of this mystery.

And this mystery is this: Jesus Christ in you, the hope of glory. The mystery that Tristan was referring to was this, the all-powerful God, all-knowing, all-present being has come to dwell in mankind—the glory of God dwelling in man. This glory God has purposed for a man to receive and to spend eternity in the very presence of God Himself, in the very Kingdom of God, a kingdom where there is no death, no sickness, no tears, no broken hearts, a kingdom filled with love, joy, peace, patience, kindness, goodness, faithfulness, gentleness, and self-control. It's a place where love is the controlling force, where love will rule in the hearts of men, and where men will learn about this all-powerful God who loves mankind with an everlasting love that is beyond our understanding. What an awesome mystery that Tristan desired to share with the world.

This next phrase Tristan wrote says the following: "Spellbinding symphony." Spellbinding, I believe Tristan was desiring to say the following with these words—that the mystery he referred to was so powerful it would capture the hearts, minds, and souls of those that would receive and believe this mystery, with such a total completeness that the only way to understand it would be by using the word *symphony*—something that comes together in such harmony it appears as a sweet sound to the ear. A symphony is a collection of many different musical instruments, which when they are played together, make a beautiful sound, as if in harmony. Those that have the privilege of hearing this sound are taken to a place of pure joy, and this joy fills the heart of those who hear. This is what I believe this precious child desired for the world to know and understand. But for as many who would receive it, they shall be made whole, complete, and lacking nothing. These are they that shall be called the children of God. These are the ones God has purposed to live the lives He has called them to.

Where Joseph gained a ring, once again, I believe this precious child shared these powerful words with the world for the following reason, but first, in order for us to understand these words, we must go into the Holy Word of God, found in the book of Genesis, which simply means the beginning. In the very first book of the Holy Bible, we can read the following story about a man named Joseph, and a ring he gained.

I try to give you, the reader, what I consider to be the best interpretation of what I believe Tristan was trying to convey or share with the world. Joseph was a young Hebrew man that was sold into slavery by his brothers because of their jealousy toward him. He had favor with God and his father, so much so that his brothers became jealous.

Upon his arrival in Egypt, he was sold to a man named Potiphar, a man who had power and authority under Pharaoh. The Egyptian kingdom at the time was considered the world power of that era. As a slave, Joseph had no rights. His life could be forfeited at the whim of his master. But Joseph gained favor in the sight of his master, and he had favor in the sight of his God. He was given complete control over his master's household, and all he did prospered.

During his time, as his master's slave, Joseph maintained his integrity, not only to his master, but also to his God. But as time went on, his master's wife desired to have a sexual relationship with Joseph, who refused to do such evil. So because of his faithfulness, not only to his master, but also to his God, this evil woman accused Joseph of trying to rape her. When his master heard this, he had Joseph thrown into prison.

Joseph spent seven years as his master's slave before he was thrown into prison. While he was in prison, two of Pharaoh's servants were thrown into prison because they displeased the Pharaoh, while they were in prison, they both had dreams. They both ended up telling their dreams to Joseph, and through the ability given to Joseph by the Lord, Joseph was able to interpret their dreams. After he interpreted their dreams, Joseph asked one of them to bring his cause before Pharaoh.

As it turned out, the one who was supposed to mention Joseph's cause before Pharaoh forgot to mention it to Pharaoh, until a time came when Pharaoh himself had a dream that disturbed him, and there was no one to interpret the dream. Then the servant that Pharaoh had thrown into prison brought up Joseph to Pharaoh, saying, "While I was in prison, there was a Hebrew slave that had the ability to interpret dreams." So Pharaoh commanded that Joseph be called from the prison, so Joseph was presented to the Pharaoh.

After Joseph interpreted the dream for Pharaoh, he was given favor by Pharaoh, raised to the position of the second behind Pharaoh in the land of Egypt, and Pharaoh himself gave unto Joseph his ring of authority, and all in the land of Egypt had to pay homage to Joseph as the authority under Pharaoh.

I believe Tristan was trying to teach the reader that faithfulness to the one true God, no matter what, will eventually result in being rewarded. We can see this truth found in the book of Hebrews 11:6, "But without faith it is impossible to please God, for he who comes to God must believe that He is; and that He is a rewarder of those that diligently seek Him."

Joseph certainly sought to seek his God, even in his times of trials and tests, and just as the Lord has promised, He rewarded Joseph in due season. In the book of Galatians 6:9, we have these words of affirmation, "And let us not grow weary while doing good, for in due season we shall reap a reward."

Today, if we remain faithful to our Master, which is the Lord and Savior Jesus Christ, He shall also bless us with favor and give us His authority to become good stewards over His possessions. But at the same time, we must remember that these possessions are His. We're just His stewards. And our Lord desires for us to be good stewards of those things He places in our care.

As we continue with what I believe Tristan desired to share and teach to this world, we can see this truth. When the favor of God is upon us. There may come a time when people will falsely accuse us of wrongdoing, and because of this, we may endure hardships that are due to things that are not of our own doing. But if we remain faithful to God, our God will bring us up out of our circumstances, and even in the midst of our circumstances, God will bless us with favor.

Just as the Lord was with Joseph, and he received God's mercy, so shall the Lord be with us when the Lord allows the enemy to come against us, not only to test our faithfulness, but also to mature our faith so we may grow into a more intimate relationship with Him. We must remember that our Lord has promised us that He will never leave us or forsake us, regardless of the circumstances we may find ourselves in.

There is a word of comfort for those of us who endure hardship when the enemy comes against us, and though we may not understand why, our Lord promises us the following, in the book of Isaiah chapter 29, verse 9, "I can hear Tristan speaking these words to all those under attack by the enemy. So shall they fear the name of the Lord from the west, and His glory from the rising of the sun; when the enemy comes in like a flood, the Spirit of the Lord will lift up a standard against him." This standard shall be greater than the flood the enemy brings against us. Our God will deliver us in our time of trial, in His perfect timing.

Our Lord desires to bless us with favor in the presence of all people. Our honor and glory comes from the Lord, and not a man. And just as God deserves the highest honor, this is what I truly believe Tristan desired to share and teach the world through these words of his.

These next words Tristan wrote are as follows, "And Paul did silence kings." Here, we have a teaching about the Apostle Paul and how the Lord worked with him and brought him into the presence of kings. So let's hear what I believe Tristan was desiring to teach us through this verse.

This story is found in the book of Acts, chapter 25. It's the story of Paul defending his faith in the Lord Jesus Christ. Paul was a prisoner of a man named Felix, a governor of Jerusalem, then after two years, Porcius Festus succeeded Felix as governor. And while Paul was under the custody of this man, he appealed unto Caesar.

Augustus was Caesar at this time in Rome. While awaiting his transfer to Rome, King Agrippa came to see Porcius Festus and was told concerning Paul. So King Agrippa desired to hear Paul's testimony concerning his faith.

In the book of Acts 25:22, we can hear the following words, "Then Agrippa said to Festus, I also would like to hear the man myself. Tomorrow he said, you shall hear him." The story continues as follows: Festus, having found no basis for the charges brought against Paul, had no words to explain to Caesar Augustus concerning Paul. His very words were as follows, "You are permitted to speak for yourself."

We also have this great promise from our God. In the book of Mark (13:9–11), we can read these words from our Lord Jesus Christ. "But watch out for yourselves, for they will deliver you up to councils, and you will be brought before rulers and kings for My sake, for a testimony to them. And the gospel must first be preached to all the nations. But when they arrest you and deliver you up, do not worry beforehand, or pre-meditate what you shall speak, but whatever is given you in that hour, speak that, for it is not you who speak, but the Holy Spirit."

I believe Tristan was referring to this teaching in our Lord's word when he wrote the following line, "And Paul did silence kings." In the book of Acts (26:1–32), Paul begins to expound on his story, and I believe that during the entire time Paul spoke, King Agrippa was silent.

Truly, how can any human speak when God Himself is speaking? I believe we, as humans, can only listen in awe as God Himself is speaking, especially when God is speaking to us personally. For the words of God are spirit, life, and power. Paul did silence kings, but only as the vessel through whom the Lord God did speak.

I also believe Tristan desired for us to know that, we also, when we are obedient and faithful to our great and awesome God, we also shall be brought into the presence of men and women of importance, those who have authority. And when we testify to the greatness of our great God, we also shall be able to silence those in authority, kings, and dignitaries.

Now, as we continue with Tristan's poem, it declares the following words: "And water became wine." We can see through these words the following teaching found in the book of John (2:1–10). I believe Tristan desired to share and teach through these words the following—the unlimited love and power our great God has for us, His children.

This teaching goes as follows—the Lord Jesus Christ and His disciples were invited to a wedding. For the most part, a wedding is a time of joy and happiness, a celebration of love between two people. According to the purpose of God, it has such great importance to God that He spoke the following words about marriage in the book of Matthew (19:3–9). Let's hear what the Word of God says.

> The Pharisees, also came to Him, testing Him, and saying to Him, 'Is it lawful for a man to divorce his wife for just any reason?' And He answered and said unto them, "Have you not read

> that He who made them at the beginning made them male and female, and said, for this reason, a man shall leave his father and mother and be joined to his wife, and the two shall become one flesh? Therefore what God has joined together, let not man separate." They said to Him, "Why then did Moses in the law, command to give a certificate of divorce, and to put her away?" He said to them, "Moses, because of the hardness of your hearts, permitted you to divorce your wives, but from the beginning, it was not so. And I say to you, whoever divorces his wife, except for sexual immorality, and marries another, commits adultery, and whoever marries her who is divorced commits adultery."

So we can see the importance that our great God places upon marriage.

As we continue with the teaching found in the book of John (2:1–10) it states the following:

> And while the Lord Jesus was there, His mother came to Him and said, they have no wine. Jesus said to her, "Woman, what does your concern have to do with Me? My hour has not yet come." His mother said to the servants, "Whatever He says to you, do it." Now there were set there six waterpots of stone, according to the manner of purification of the Jews, containing twenty or thirty gallons apiece, Jesus said to them, "Fill the waterpots with water, and they filled them to the brim." And He said to them, "Draw some out now, and they took it to the master of the feast," and they took it. When the master of the feast had tasted the water that was made wine and did not know where it came from

[but the servants who had drawn the wine knew], the master of the feast called the bridegroom, and said to him, "Every man at the beginning sets out the good wine," and when the guests have well drunk, then the inferior. "You have kept the good wine until now."

So let's hear what I believe Tristan was attempting to teach and share with the world through the following when he wrote, "And water became wine." We learn through God's word how important marriage is to our God. He desires for us to love, honor, and respect our spouses. Both husbands and wives are to do this.

The Lord Himself honors the marriage relationship. When the water became wine, the Lord declares this to be the beginning of signs our Lord Jesus Christ did in Cana of Galilee and manifested His glory, and His disciples believed in Him. I believe Tristan wanted to share with us this truth. Our God desires to bless our lives with miracles when we honor our God through the marriage relationship.

It's our obedience to our Lord's word that brings about the miracles in our lives that our Lord desires to bring about in our lives. As the teaching continues, we can see that not only does our Lord desires to bless our lives, but just as the water turned into wine was the very best, that our Lord desires for us to receive the very best from Him, so it is with us.

The Lord desires for us to receive the very best life has to offer. We can see this truth found in the book of John 10:10, where our Lord's word declares the following,

> The thief does not come except to steal and to kill, and to destroy, I have come that they might have life, and that life they may have it more abundantly. "Our Lord promises us the very best that life has to offer. This is what I believe Tristan wanted to teach and share with the world."

As we continue with Tristan's next verse, we read these words, "And angels did merry-fly."

There are a few verses in our Lord's word where we're told that the Lord sent His angels to minister unto mankind. We have this teaching in our Lord's word found in the book of Matthew 4:11 and hear the Word of God, "Then the devil left Him, and behold angels came and ministered to Him."

Also, we have the following teaching in the book of John 1:51.

> And He said to him, most assuredly, I say to you hereafter you shall see heaven open, and the angels of God ascending and descending upon the Son of man.

I believe Tristan was referring to the teaching that is found in the book of Hebrews 1:14.

> Are they not all ministering spirits sent forth to minister for those who will inherit salvation?

So I believe that what Tristan was trying to share and teach with the world was the following when he wrote, "And angels merry-fly." That the Lord has appointed His angels to come to our aid and minister to those of us that will inherit salvation. And I believe that when our Lord's angels are sent to the aid of one of our Lord's brother's or sister's, then I believe His angels are filled with delight to be able to serve the Lord God in this manner. I believe that they are filled with joy to come to our aid. So I believe that what Tristan was trying to convey to the world is the joy and delight the angels of God experience when they merry fly to our assistance.

As we continue with Tristan's poem, we come to this line that states the following, "And dead were raised amazed." Again, we can find more than a couple of our Lord's teachings, which refer to those that were dead being brought back to life, or as Tristan said, were raised amazed. I also believe that those who witnessed our Lord bringing back the dead to life were also amazed. Let's look at three different teachings from our Lord's word that teaches us about the dead being raised, as Tristan stated, amazed.

The first is found in the book of Mark 5:42. Let's heat our Lord's word. While He was still speaking some came from the ruler of the synagogue's house who said, "Your daughter is dead, why trouble the Teacher any further?"

As soon as Jesus heard the word that was spoken, He said to the ruler of the synagogue, "Do not be afraid, only believe." And He permitted no one to follow Him except Peter, James, and John the brother of James. Then He came to the house of the ruler of the synagogue and saw a tumult and those who wept and wailed loudly. When He came in He said to them, "Why make this commotion and weep? The child is not dead but sleeping." And they ridiculed Him. But when He had put them all outside, He took the father and mother of the child and those who were with Him and entered where the child was lying. Then He took the child by the hand, and said to her, "Talitha, Cumi [which is translated, "Little girl, I say to you arise"]. Immediately the girl arose and walked, for she was twelve years of age. And they were overcome with great amazement. But He commanded them strictly that no one should know it and said that something should be given her to eat.

We can see in this teaching, not only the truth of our Lord's Word, but the truth of Tristan's poem line, "And the dead were raised amazed." Not only was this child amazed at her coming back from the dead, but the people who saw her brought back to life were also greatly amazed.

The next teaching about the dead being raised and the astonishment it brought forth is found in the book of Luke 7:11–17. Let's hear our Lord's word.

> Now it happened, the day after, that He went into a city called Nain, and many of His disciples went with Him and a large crowd. And when He came near the gate of the city, behold a dead man was being carried out. The only son of his mother; and she was a widow, and a large

crowd from the city was with her. When the Lord saw her, He had compassion on her and said to her, "Do not weep." Then He came and touched the coffin, and those that carried him stood still. And He said, "Young man, I say to you, arise." So he who was dead sat up and began to speak. And He presented him to his mother. Then fear came upon all, and they glorified God, saying, "A great prophet has risen among us, and the Lord God has visited His people." And this report about Him went throughout all Judea and all the surrounding region.

Here's one more teaching about how being raised from the dead amazed people. We can see that, at least, this man's mother was surely amazed at her son being brought back from the dead. As I'm sure that the man himself was amazed at his return to life. When I give it some thought, it amazes me. I'm sure most, if not all, people who witness someone being brought back from the dead would be greatly amazed. If I myself were not a follower of Jesus Christ, I myself would be amazed—just being honest. In this teaching, we see the words, "Then fear came upon all, and they glorified God."

The word *fear* here is defined as being afraid. In this verse, what seems to me unusual, is that the Jewish had in the Old Testament teachings about people that were raised from the dead, so why were they afraid? I believe that when we as humans see the power of God, it can only cause us as humans to be afraid of this all-powerful being, who we can understand as He who controls all things.

Most of the people who have had an encounter with the one true God were filled with fear, which I translate as awe. Having a godly experience most people are led to glorify God for His awesomeness. These people glorified God when the young man was brought back from the dead. This is what I believe Tristan was trying to share with the world when he wrote, "And dead were raised amazed."

The third teaching we find in the Lord's holy word is found in the book of John (11:1–44). A very long passage, but nevertheless, it has a great teaching for us to receive. In our Lord's word about the dead being brought back to life, let's hear the Word of God.

> Now a certain man was sick, Lazarus of Bethany, the town of Mary and her sister Martha, it was that Mary who anointed the Lord with fragrant oil and wiped His feet with her hair. Whose brother Lazarus was sick.
> Therefore, the sisters sent to Him, saying, "Lord, behold, he whom you love is sick." When Jesus heard that, He said, "This sickness is not unto death. But for the glory of God, that the Son of God may be glorified through it." Now, Jesus loved Martha and her sister and Lazarus. So, when He heard that he was sick, He stayed for two more days in the place where He was.
> Then after this, He said to the disciples, "Let us go into Judea again." The disciples said to Him, "Rabbi, lately the Jews sought to stone you, and are you going there again?" Jesus answered, "Are there not twelve hours in the day? If anyone walks in the day, he does not stumble, because he sees the light of this world. But if one walks in the night, he stumbles, because the light is not in him. These things," He said, and after that, He said to them, "Our friend Lazarus sleeps, but I go that I may wake him up."
> Then His disciples said, "Lord, if he sleeps he will get well." However, Jesus spoke of his death. But they thought that He was speaking about taking rest in sleep. Then Jesus said to them, plainly, "Lazarus is dead, and I am glad for your sakes that I was not there, that you may believe. Nevertheless let us go to him." Then Thomas, who is called the twin, said to his fellow disciples, "Let us also go that we may die with Him." So

when Jesus came, He found that he had already been in the tomb for four days now. Bethany was near Jerusalem, about two miles away.

And many of the Jews had joined the women around Martha and Mary, to comfort them concerning their brother. Now Martha, as soon as she heard that Jesus was coming, went and met Him, but Mary was sitting in the house. Now Martha said to Jesus, "Lord, if you had been here, my brother would not have died, but even now I know that whatever you ask of God, God will give you." Jesus said to her, "Your brother will rise again." Martha said to Him, "I know that he will rise again in the resurrection on the last day."

Jesus said to her, "I am the resurrection, and the life, he who believes in Me, though he may die, he shall live, and whoever lives and believes in Me shall never die, do you believe this?" She said to Him, "Yes, Lord, I believe that you are the Christ, the Son of God, who is to come into the world."

And when she had said these things, she went her way and secretly called Mary her sister, saying, "The teacher has come and is asking for you." As soon as she heard that, she arose quickly and came to Him. Now Jesus had not yet come into the town but was in the place where Martha met Him.

Then the Jews who were with her in the house, and comforting her, when they saw that Mary rose up quickly, and went out, followed her, saying she is going to the tomb to weep there. Then, when Mary came where Jesus was, and saw Him, she fell down at His feet, saying to Him, "Lord if you had been here my brother would not have died." Therefore, when Jesus saw her weeping, He groaned in the spirit and was troubled. And He said, where have they laid him?

They said to Him, "Lord, come and see." Jesus wept. Then the Jews said, "See how He loved him?" And some of them said, "Could not this man, who opened the eyes of the blind, also have kept this man from dying?" Then Jesus, groaning in Himself, came to the tomb. It was a cave, and a stone lay against it. Jesus said, "Take away the stone." Martha, the sister of him who was dead, said to Him, "Lord, by this time there is a stench, for he has been dead four days." Jesus said to her, "Did I not say to you, that if you would believe you would see the glory of God?"

Then they took away the stone from the place where the dead man was lying, and Jesus lifted up His eyes and said, "Father, I thank you that you have heard Me, and I know that you always hear Me. But because of the people who are standing by I said this, that they may believe that you sent Me." Now when He had said these things, He cried out in a loud voice, "Lazarus come forth." And he who died came out bound hand and foot with graveclothes, and his face was wrapped with a cloth, Jesus said to them, "Loose him and let him go."

Here I believe is just one of the greatest teachings about the dead being raised and amazed. Lazarus had been in the grave for four days and yet at the Lord's command was brought back to life. Can you imagine his amazement?

And I believe that Tristan desired to share this point with the world—that not only were Lazarus's sisters amazed at his rising from the dead, but that those that were with them were also amazed, and our Lord desired to show us the glory of God. All we have to do is believe. This is what I believe Tristan wanted to share with the world when he wrote, "And the dead were raised amazed."

As we continue with Tristan's poem, we come to the next line, which states the following, "And empty was the grave." This teaching, which I believe Tristan wanted to share with the world, is found in the Matthew 27:50–53. Let's hear the word of the Lord. This teaches us the following:

> And Jesus cried out again with a loud voice, and yielded His spirit, then, behold, the veil of the temple was torn from the top of the veil, to the bottom, and the earth quaked, and the rocks were split, and the graves were opened, and many of the saints who had been asleep were raised, and coming out of the graves after His resurrection, they went into the Holy City, and appeared to many.

So here, we can see through this teaching that what our Lord's word shows us is that those that were in the graves were raised and came up out of their graves, and also went into the Holy City and appeared to many, after the Lords' resurrection. This, I believe, is what Tristan was trying and desiring to share with the world—that the grave has no power to hold those that are believers in the Lord Jesus Christ. So this is what I believe Tristan meant when he wrote the following words, "And empty was the grave."

The next line in Tristan's poem is "Is the step." A short line, but what I believe is to be of great importance. I believe that what Tristan desired to say with these words is that the journey that one begins to take when he or she has made a decision to accept Jesus Christ as their Lord and Savior, to follow the teachings of Jesus Christ, is a great decision. It's the step that leads a person from one form of life to another, a step that can forever change one's life.

This is what I believe Tristan desired to share with the world. It just takes one step to begin this journey with the one true God, but our Lord is waiting for us to take that first step, then He can come in and do the work that is necessary for us to receive all the promises in His holy word.

This next line in Tristan poem goes as follows: "That takes one's breath." This line from Tristan's poem, I believe, was said in the following context after one has decided to follow Jesus Christ as Lord and Savior. Their experience will be one of such awe and wonder that it can only take away one's breath. It's so overwhelming that one is left in awe of the greatness of the Lord.

And now, we come to the last verse in Tristan's poem, which states the following, "When miracles manifest." I believe that what Tristan wanted to teach and share with the world is that these words are the greatest in his poem. When he wrote these words, "When miracles manifest," we as human beings, have the greatest miracles happen in our lives when our Lord blesses us with the precious gift of life every day.

When we fall asleep at the end of each day, and our Lord blesses us with the gift of life in the morning when we wake, our response should be thankfulness. The first words our Lord speaks to us are these, "I love you, precious child. You are my beloved, the apple of my eye." These words are found in the book of Deuteronomy 32:10. Let's hear the Word of God.

> He found him in a desert land, and in the wasteland, a howling wilderness. He encircled him, He instructed him, He kept him as the apple of His eye.

This is just one aspect of our Lords' love for us all. Here is what I believe Tristan desired to share with the world. The interpretation of these words are as follows—our great God comes and finds us when we are in our greatest need for Him, when life has beaten us down, when we were in such a condition, that we felt unworthy to be loved by anyone, especially by the one true God. But our Lord declares that He encircles us, embraces us in His arms, and then teaches us the life He has purposed for us to live. And then He keeps us as His most precious treasure.

We also have these words in Psalms 17:8. Let's hear the Word of God. Our Lord declares the following:

> Keep me as the apple of your eye, hide me under the shadow of your wings.

Here, we have the teaching that we ourselves can ask the Lord to keep us as the apple of His eye, to keep us under His protection. Let's look at a promise found in 1 John 5:14–15.

> Now this is the confidence that we have in Him, that if we ask anything according to His will, He hears us, and if we know that He hears us, whatever we ask, we know that we have the petitions that we have asked of Him.

So we know it is our Lords' will for us to be the apple of His eye. We have another verse with the words "The apple of His eye." It's found in the book of Zechariah 2:8, and the Lords' word declares the following:

> For thus says the Lord of Hosts, He sent me after glory, to the nations which plunder you, for he who touches you, touches the apple of His eye.

Here, we have the promise that whosoever is your enemy, he that plunders you, if they so much as touch you, they are touching the apple of God's eye. You are the very precious treasure of the living God. You belong to the Lord. Our great God keeps and protects you as the apple of His eye, a most peculiar treasure, a treasure of such great value that God the Father has sent His one and only begotten Son, that through Him and His sacrifice, may save the world. And once again mankind can be reconciled to the one true God.

These next words, His beloved, are found in a few verses in our Lord's Holy word. I believe Tristan desired to share with the world the following—Gods' great love for mankind. The book of Song of Solomon, for most of this book, describes the love relationship between two people, a love that teaches us that this is the best relationship that can develop between two people, one where both parties can only call each other, my beloved. It's a love that is so rich for one another that the only way to describe their love for one another is to use the words, my beloved.

Another place where the Lord uses the phrase "my beloved" is found in the book of Daniel 9:23. Let's hear the Word of God that He declares in His word.

> At the beginning of your supplications the command went out, and I have come to tell you, for you are greatly beloved, Therefore, consider the matter, and understand the vision.

This is what I believe Tristan wanted to share with the world. He desired for us to know that God Himself calls us His beloved. We are God's beloved, His very precious treasure. We're so special to our Lord He Himself will send an angel to confirm His word to us.

Now, I will start to write about Tristan's religious writings. I believe Tristan was very intelligent when it involved expounding on the Word of God. As you'll soon see. His first titled writing is called "Truth Teaching"—the proverbs of Solomon, Son of David!

This teaching is found in the book of Proverbs 1:1–19, and let's hear the Word of God, the proverbs of Solomon, the son of David, king of Israel.

> To know wisdom and instruction; to perceive the words of understanding; To receive the instruction of wisdom, justice, and judgment, and equity; To give subtilty to the simple, to the young man knowledge and discretion. A wise man will increase learning, and a man of understanding shall attain unto wise counsels; To understand a proverb, and the interpretation; the words of the wise, and their dark sayings. The

> fear of the Lord is the beginning of knowledge, but fools despise wisdom and instruction. My son, hear the instruction of thy Father, and forsake not the law of thy Mother; For they shall be an ornament of grace unto thy head, and chains about thy neck.
>
> My son, if sinners entice thee, consent thou not. If they say, come with us, let us wait for blood let us lurk privily for the innocent without cause; let us swallow them up alive as the grave; and whole, as those that go down to the pit; We shall find all precious substance, we shall fill our houses with spoil. Cast in thy lot among us; let us all have one purse. My son. walk not thou in the way with them, refrain thy foot from their path; For their feet run to evil, and make haste to shed blood. Surely in vain, the net is spread in the sight of any bird. And they lay wait for their own blood; they lurk privily for their own lives. So are the ways of every one that is greedy of gain; which taketh away the life of the owners thereof.

I believe that Tristan was expressing his belief in the truth he found in God's word. He truly believed it was of the utmost importance to understand God's word concerning the instruction of His Father. His faith is shown by the words he just expressed in the book of Solomon. First, we need to look at the word *proverbs* and its meaning.

Proverbs simply means words of wisdom spoken by a being that has all wisdom, or a fair amount of wisdom. And ultimately, all words of wisdom come from God. Tristan's heart received the truth of God's word as truth. His faith has been shown by his writing these words, for if one did not believe, then why would he write concerning a subject he really didn't believe in?

Most of the next few writings of Tristan's will be focused on his religious, spiritual learning and understanding of God's word. I pray that these writings can help others understand God more intimately, but also, for those who read this, to have a better understanding of who Tristan was.

The first writing I desire to share with you is titled "Reflections on Scripture," seeking whom He may devour! One of the most monumental accomplishments of mankind is to know something and still not believe it. The ancient Greek philosopher Pythagoras told his students that to be taught is to believe, but to experience is to know absolutely. So let me ask you, first, assuming that this maxim…this ancient aphorism is correct,(which it is), say for example, do you know that you're alive because you were taught this, thus, it becomes your belief? Or do you know that you're alive because you are experiencing it? The latter being obviously the objective truth to the collective whole.

Assuming it's the latter, yet we experience a miracle daily. We experience the creation, the life, and the purpose, and the unavoidable continuum of the drama of good and evil. You experience this truth, and I don't have to tell you that.

But we in this present generation tend to deny these things as significant in our lives in order to support the platforms of a stubborn, right-wing, atheistic foundation, which the superstructure thereof further protects from a total systematic meltdown of the superego (the psychoanalytical model of Jung/Freud that is theorized to either reward, also to punish, through a system of moral attitudes, conscience, and a sense of guilt). Had we not abandoned our religious faith and spiritual inclinations? I'm saying it's curiously convenient to be an atheist if you have an extreme disposition to do evil or even have a complacent apathetic spiritual demeanor. It becomes palatable. Left and right—the political left and right, liberal and conservative, respectively, thus applied as a subtitle of atheist, Christian, or whatever.

I only use these to contrast the differences in extremes of potential for modification, change, or the lack thereof. Hence, many in our generation (the late seventies) seem to be easily rocked to sleep by the traditional, old-fashioned, a simple uncomplicated tendency to not progress, to just worship science, to follow Charles Darwin and find not within the thing created, the signature of the creator.

Progressive collective spiritual development and awareness is in my mind—the religio-political left, a liberalistic/liberal, tolerant, open-minded, washed-up conservative/right-wing, atheistic, indoctrination. You know, that there is a creator, by using reasonable deduction.

The evidence is the creation. To all my friends still struggling with the atheistic indoctrination…do not be lulled to sleep. Hear the following words found in 1 Peter 5:8.

> Be sober, be vigilant, because the devil walks about like a roaring lion, seeking whom he may devour.

I hopefully pray that the following writing by Tristan would touch the hearts and minds and spirits of those that read these words of his. I will do my best to give you, the reader, what I believe Tristan wanted to share with the world with this writing.

Tristan starts this teaching off with these awesome words that we, as human beings, have come to bring about in our lives the following truth—to know something, and still not believe it. I believe this is the truth Tristan is referring to here—that we, as mankind, have been given the following information. It's been made available to all mankind, that all of creation has been created by a creator, and this creator is called God.

Every culture known to mankind has had one type of or form of a being they called god or gods. So most of mankind knows about this information, yet we still don't believe it. I believe this is a very sad situation for a man to be in—to know something and still not believe it.

Tristan states the following from the Greek philosopher Pythagoras—he taught his students or his followers this teaching—"To be taught, is to believe, but to experience something is to know absolutely." Tristan teaches that if this ancient aphorism is correct (which it is) according to his belief, I believe that most of this teaching can be true. But not in every situation. I believe that the latter part of this teaching is absolutely true. When we experience something, we cannot deny this truth.

But on the other side of this teaching, we see that to be taught is to believe. I don't agree. Tristan wrote the following. He stated that we say to someone, "Do you know that you're alive because you have been taught this. If so, then it thus becomes your belief." But what if someone taught you on the subject of UFOs? No matter how much of their teaching you receive, you still don't believe.

Using Tristan's last phrase in this teaching, he states the following—to experience something is to know absolutely. But, what if I were to experience a life of sixty years here on earth? Would this experience convince me I was alive? Or would I know this absolutely? I would know absolutely.

A better example to use would be religion. For example, if one were taught God's word completely, one might come to believe, but even after being taught God's word, one could still choose not to believe. But what if one experienced God? One would know absolutely who God is—that He is who He says He is. This is just one example. It can be applied to all religions. Tristan also said the following about Pythagoras's teaching, that the latter being obviously the objective truth to the collective whole; assuming the latter.

Tristan continues his teaching by saying and expressing these words, yet we experience a miracle daily. We experience the creation, which is ourselves, and all the wonderful aspects the creation experiences—the ability or gift of healing the creation performs upon itself. The ability or gift to love others unconditionally, then we have the gift of the mind. This gift alone is beyond our ability to comprehend.

Just to give thought to all that man has accomplished by using his mind is awesome in itself, yet we still experience life and purpose, and the unavoidable continuum of the drama of good and evil. All of us as mankind have experienced these things and continue to experience them, as Tristan said. He doesn't have to tell you this.

Tristan goes on to say we as a generation today tend to deny that these things have any true significance in our lives, in order to support the platforms of a stubborn, hardhearted, right-wing, atheistic foundation, which, in reference to the superstructure thereof, further protects from a total systematic meltdown of the superego. Have we not abandoned our religious faith and spiritual inclinations?

Tristan stated that to him, it's curiously convenient for mankind, in general, to be an atheist if mankind has an extreme disposition to do evil, or for a man to have a complacent, apathetic spiritual demeanor. It becomes palatable, left and right—the political left and right, liberal or conservative, respectfully, thus applied as a subtitle of atheist, Christian, or whatever. Tristan, here, is saying the following—he is only using this to contrast the difference in extremes of "potential" for modification, change, or the lack thereof.

Hence, many of our generation, the late seventies, seem to be easily rocked to sleep by the traditional, old-fashioned, simple, uncomplicated tendency to not progress. This simply means we are lazy, as far as seeking to improve our lives by embracing the greatest gift given to man, by which man may live out his life with the greatest benefits given to man for his use.

Most of mankind seems to worship science or Darwin and find not within the thing created, the signature of the creator. It simply states that we look to ourselves and yet refuse to accept God for who He is.

Progressive, collective spiritual development and awareness is in our minds. But Tristan states that we face what he refers to as the religio-political left, which is a liberalistic, tolerant, open-minded view that refuses to be rocked to complacent sleep by an obsolete old-fashioned, conservative/right-wing, atheistic indoctrination. Tristan merely states here that we all have within us this desire to know God. He's saying, for himself, that he will not be deceived by the false indoctrination that comes from a man that leads men away from God. He states that you know there is a God, that there is a creator, you only have to use reasonable deduction. The evidence is the creation.

To all my friends still struggling with atheistic indoctrination, do not be lulled to sleep. Tristan closes this teaching by quoting from the book of 1 Peter 5:8, which says the following:

> Be sober, be vigilant, because your adversary the devil, walks about like a roaring lion, seeking whom he may devour.

Simply stated, we are to do our very best to stay alert to the attacks of the enemy, which he brings against you to destroy your life. May these words of Tristan touch your hearts as they touched mine.

This next writing of Tristan's is again a writing on "reflections on scripture." This one is entitled "Et Lux Tenebris Lucet." The following are Tristan's thoughts on this subject. He starts off by saying,

> I was thinking about you the other day, just as I have every single day of your life, isn't this a most beautiful thing to say to another being? My mother, Angie, said this to me the other day in a letter recently, and to those of you who know her, it will come as no surprise, for as my brother Trevor told me, "Tris, we have the sweetest mom in the world, don't you agree?" Of course, I do, as would most people out there who know my mom, she has never let me down.

Now, in the New Testament, there's a teaching found in the book of John 1:45–49, which teaches us how well our Lord Jesus Christ knows us as individuals. Let's hear the Word of God.

> Phillip found Nathanael and said to him, we have found Him of whom Moses in the law, also the prophets wrote, Jesus of Nazareth, the son of Joseph. And Nathanael said to him, "Can anything good come out of Nazareth?" Phillip said to him, "Come and see." Jesus saw Nathanael coming towards Him, and said of him, "An Israelite indeed, in whom is no deceit." Nathanael said to Him, "How do you know me?" Jesus answered and said to him, "Before Phillip called you, when you were under the fig tree, I saw you." Nathanael answered and said to Him, "Rabbi, you are the Son of God, you are the King of Israel."

We can see through this teaching the following—first, we can see that our great God has blessed us with the privilege to know our Lord and Savior Jesus Christ. With these words, we can see this truth that Phillip, upon meeting Jesus Christ, for some reason, recognized Jesus for who He was. For in his statement to Nathanael, he declares the following, "We have found Him whom Moses in the law, and also the prophets, wrote…Jesus of Nazareth." In Deuteronomy 18:15–19, we can hear this word from God,

> The Lord thy God will raise up unto thee a prophet from the midst of thee, of thy brethren, like unto me, unto Him shall ye hearken.
>
> According to all that thou desirest of the Lord thy God in Horeb, in the day of the assembly, saying, Let me not hear again the voice of the Lord my God, neither let me see this great fire anymore, that I die not. And the Lord said unto me, they have well spoken that which they have spoken. I will raise them up a prophet from among their brethren, like unto thee, and will put My words in His mouth, and He shall speak unto them all that I shall command Him. And it shall come to pass, that whoever will not hearken unto My words which He shall speak in My name, I will require it of him.

God, the Father, has purposed for us to know Him. He spoke this truth a long time ago to Moses, and down through the years through the prophets, and then He sent His only begotten Son, the Lord Jesus Christ, so we as mankind could have the opportunity and the privilege of knowing our God.

As Tristan's teaching continues, we can read the following words by Tristan.

> When the word God is used, though in the English language is singular, it is a noun that has

a masculine connotation. This was not the original word used by the Jewish people. This word has been translated from the Hebrew word for the creator of all things. The original word used by the Jewish people was the word *Elohim*, which is explained as neither male nor female, but perfect unity, and plural.

That's right, the word *Elohim* is plural. We can see this truth in God's word in Genesis 1:26. Let's hear the Word of God.

> And God said, let us make man in our image, after our likeness. But understand, like a plural in the singular. It expresses the mystery and absolute un-comprehensible state of the deity, one God/creator, who manifests a triple countenance. But I will write and expound on this in a later lecture.

Science, logic, and reason can only march so far victoriously before they fall face first upon their own spears. They do this at the feet of Him who transcends science, logic, and reason. In fact, at the feet of the one who ordained science, logic, and reason, and subordinated them to His word and to His will. It is only when these three—science, logic, and reason—deviate from their intended purpose and attempt to exalt themselves against the knowledge of God that they lose their dignity. That said, take this as an example, we have heard it said that cause and effect are a law of sorts.

When scientists talk about the origin of the universe and proposed different theories, cause and effect seem to be always in operation. But when we theoretically trace far enough back, even before the big bang, we may ask, how did He come to be?

Yes, it may be true that the Lord ordained the big bang, but we still want to know how did the Lord come to be. Did the Lord have a creator? No. And if He did, then the sequence would go on and on and on, into eternity, of who made who (ironically, that title was an AC/DC song, and how fitting for a spiritually benumbed rock band).

So what we have here is now a brick wall, whereupon cause and effect crashes and is no more. And here's why and how. The Lord cannot and will not be explained by the lesser operations He put into existence, which rule our lives. And furthermore, have you ever tried to wrap your mind around that concept *how* something can always *be*. It's very difficult, right?

Of course, a finite mind cannot comprehend the infinite. Come on, all of you who consider yourselves to be smart and intelligent people, must you have to have an answer for everything? Seriously, it's almost as if the Lord is saying to us, "Hey, people, really now, can I have just this one issue? That I am who I say I am? Just this one mystery, please.

No, not really of course, but I will remind you of what the Lord spoke to Job, found in Job 38:2. Let's hear what our Lord declares.

> Who is this that darkeneth counsel by words without knowledge?

In essence or in truth, our great God is saying, "Job, your just a man of limited understanding, how can it be possible that you of limited understanding are trying to understand that which has an unlimited existence?" And again, our great God teaches us the following about Himself found in Isaiah 58:8–9. Let's hear the words of our Lord.

> "For my thoughts are not your thoughts, neither are your ways my ways," saith the Lord.

Also our Lord teaches us the following in Proverbs 3:5,

> Trust in the Lord with all your heart, and lean not unto thine own understanding.

Again, the Lord declares the following in His word in Job 38:4–5,

> "Where was thou when I laid the foundations of the earth? Declare, if thou has understand-

ing. Who hath laid the measures thereof, if thou knowest? Or who has stretched the line upon it?

And again, our great God declares the following in Job 38:33. We hear these words from our Lord,

> Knowest thou the ordinances of heaven? canst thou set the dominion thereof in the earth?

Tristan then states the following,

> Mom, I will begin to free-style some of our Lord's scriptures for a few minutes. There are many more scriptures just like these, but suffice it to say that my point is this, that all of mankind should humble themselves before the Lord, before His infinite mystery.
> How fitting for a man to attempt to figure, surmise, and calculate such divine mysteries, when five minutes from now, man will be lusting after the next television celebrity, or begin telling vain lies while drinking hard alcohol on the Lord's holy day.

Really now, people, we can't even figure out how to control or master our own lives for one complete day, yet we claim, all of us, to be authorities on divine matters. And we allow these stumbling blocks to cause great harm and destruction to our faith. Tristan states that he will spend a few minutes here to give us some examples to think about.

> It has been said more than once by mankind that after we have succeeded in this life that all these things shall be revealed to us. Until then, let us ponder some earthly things, such as, the cause and effect of why we can't get out of debt, or why

we can't keep and maintain a good relationship with others. Peace to all of you, until the next time.

This next writing of Tristan's is titled "The Lectures," what Tristan calls the blueprint. What is it? This is what Tristan desired to share with the world, a series of videos that would be about twenty to twenty-five minutes long to be lectures to be displayed on YouTube and Facebook for untold numbers to see and view, given to various aspects of God's holy word.

The Nature of the One True God, the Created Universe, and The Fabric of Reality was to be released sometime between 2016 and 2017. Tristan intended to have this done by having his mom record him in their home. Tristan would be giving discourses on the following subjects:

1. How God can be self-existent, and man's limited faculties of comprehension.
2. Prophecies about Jesus Christ found in the old testament of the Holy Bible.
3. The marriage of science and religion, reconstructing old paradigms.
4. Free will and accountability, in relation to why bad things happen to good people—the fabric of reality.
5. Particle physics and quantum theory, where this all fits in.
6. Pagan heresies and alleged contradictions, whose arguments I have totally crushed—the silencing of atheism.
7. The Holy Trinity—how to see and perceive this truth manifested in the Holy Bible and how to understand it.

Tristan writes the following: "I will open each of these lectures with a prayer. For blessing and understanding, and for blessings to all who view these videos with an open mind." Tristan also states the following at the end of this writing,

> Mom, we will start here with these seven topics, and we'll see what kind of success or responses we receive from the world. I would like to get the attention of Creflo Dollar, or T. D. Jakes (just aiming high). But we will see anyway. This is your copy of the blueprint, save this. Tell my brother, Trevor, about this idea. I believe this is big time brilliant mom. Let it be known in the Facebook file what I plan to do. Love you, Tristan.

Tristan's next writing states the following:

> Mom, post this poem and the religious post I wrote on the other paper. Together, as soon as you can. I love you.
>
> Hello, Mom, I love you! Well, guess what? Kathy Shaw wrote me such a nice letter, so encouraging. I've enclosed it. I would like for you to read it, to see what a good person she is, Mom. She is another person who has always been my friend and has never done me any harm. Never! Always flattered me as a matter of fact. As a friend, I love her.
>
> Anyway, I've also included in here, what is a religious post that I would like for you to post, please. Of course, it's by me, and somewhat funny also, I think. You will like it too! Also, please post this short poem with it. Thank you. I love you. You're in my prayers strongly.

I have no idea what Tristan titled this poem, but I will share his writing.

> Where light pierces the heart quite blinding,
> And where treasures await their finding,
> Tis where He whispers softly…"write"
> Wherefore these poems are born tonight!
> This pen of mine a supernatural wand;
> In truth give not much thought upon,
> For in my hand, It's life its own,
> I touch, it writes… That's all that's known.
> The miracle of Solomon's great ring,
> Sealed upon me… This secret thing.
> And on my side, the King of Kings…
> Of whom I seek to please in all things,
> And all who read these poems of mine,
> For if indeed I made you smile…
> Then it has been worth my while.
> In His Name!
>
> Sincerely,
> Tristan Ray Thompson

This next writing by Tristan is titled "Reflections on Scripture." He first starts this writing as follows,

> Post this, Mom, ASAP. Store on Facebook, information file also, and save. As you know, the world needs to see this… Put it into cyberspace.

Recently, in various discussions with some people, over two specific instances of God's miracles attributed to "Yeshua" or in the Greek translation, if you prefer, "Jesus," I've come to this conclusion, mind you now, my attitude is not about "if," but rather "why"!

The fig tree parable, found in Matthew 21:22. What is the Lord desiring to teach us concerning this parable about the fig tree? Let's hear the word of the Lord.

> Now in the morning, as He returned into the city, He was hungry. And when He saw a fig tree in the way, He came to it and found there nothing thereon but leaves, and said unto it, "Let no fruit grow on you ever again." Immediately the fig-tree withered away. And when the disciples saw it, they marveled, saying, how soon is the fig-tree withered away. Jesus answered and said unto them, "Verily I say unto you, if ye have faith and doubt not, ye shall not only do this which is done to the fig-tree, but also if ye shall say unto this mountain, be thou removed, and be thou cast into the sea, it shall be done. And all things whatsoever, ye shall ask in prayer, believing, ye shall receive."

We can see through this teaching that the Lord Jesus Christ is hungry and that coming upon the fig tree, He found nothing on it. He pronounces what seems to be a curse upon the fig tree—that the tree shall no longer produce fruit thereon, and the fig tree withered away. And His disciples marveled at how quickly the fig tree withered away.

God spoke about our Lord Jesus Christ's coming to the world, so the world might be saved. God spoke this prophetic word to Adam and Eve when they rebelled against God's law. We can see this truth found in Genesis 3:15. Let's hear the Lord's word.

> And I will put enmity between you and the woman, and between your seed and her seed, He shall bruise your head, and you shall bruise His heel.

Here, when the Lord God spoke these words, He was referring to the fact that mankind needed a savior and that He would provide one that would defeat the enemy. It was our Lord and Savior Jesus

Christ, the Messiah, He who would offer to mankind the gift of salvation.

And the singular aspect of the reference to the woman is in reference to the Virgin Mary, who gave birth to our Lord and Savior, Jesus Christ. So we can see that our great God has purposed and that He desires for us to know our great and awesome Lord and Savior Jesus Christ.

Tristan continues his writings by stating the following:

> Now, in the New Testament, the Lord Jesus Christ teaches one of His early disciples all about himself in one short sentence, and also that He "saw" him at a time when the said disciple was alone in a certain place. Thus demonstrating His supernatural power and knowledge concerning all things, such as the "Disciple" poem I recently posted on Facebook. Quantum theory and quantum physics, which also manifest in my writings. So "esoteric" poetry because not just anyone can understand or appreciate it without being "initiated" into the "greater mysteries" or having a super mundane knowledge, or unless you are illuminated by the Holy Spirit.
>
> Some of you may know me, superficially only, my past crimes I've committed, my substance abuse, whatever. I am not, however, the sum total of my flaws. However, once saying that, we must fail often to succeed only once.
>
> But now, I'm buried with Christ Jesus, through submersion of the baptismal waters, where I am raised to new life through grace by faith (and works), and now, transcending out of and above the "base metals" of the carnal nature. I strive to achieve the completion of the spiritual alchemical process of becoming that philosophical gold of the alchemist beholding the "midnight sun." The one lovingly thinking about you every

day, every single moment and day of your life, even before you were born here upon the earth.

In the book of John 17:24, we can read these words, "Just as He chose us in Him before the foundation of the world, that we should be Holy and without blame before Him in love." So here, we may learn that even before the foundation of the world, we were in the heart and thoughts of our great God. All this before the foundation of the world. All this before we were born here upon the earth. [Tristan states that we should just jump out there and say that!] Now, let's ask ourselves, What do we think about most of the time? Whoa! Scary, Huh?

That's right, we all could blush on that one. My name is Tristan Ray Thompson, and I have easily out sinned you. Yeah, I fall short, but God's word states the following in the book of Romans 3:23, "For all have sinned and fall short of the glory of God." But out of love, I continue to strive, to transcend what I call this, my own madness and selfishness. I desire to attain to a greater power and purpose for my life. Thank you, Mom, for the loving words that inspired this writing today.

Tristan wrote the following poem titled "Et Lux Tenebris Lucet."

A spark from the divine flame,
Shineth in the dark,
Deeply feeling, born from love,
To teach, heal, touch, rhyme, write,
Tristan Ray, my earthly name,
The light born from the spark…

Rhyming words dispel the dark with poetic delight! Spellbinding unto the heart, blinding to the sight, this is the supernatural, cast but through the Holy Spirit's might. Comprehend this quickly, you must, before the time takes flight.

"Et Lux Tenebris Lucet," Forever the light!
(And the light shineth in the dark)

By: Tristan Ray Thompson
04-11-2015

Note from author to be posted with this: Anyone who reads the reflections on scripture that preceded this poem and has questions surfacing about all the bad in the world and how that lines up with what I'm saying, please look for my next posting, a week from now, about free will and accountability/"The Fabric of Reality."

By: Tristan Ray Thompson

This next writing that I will share from Tristan is dated February 28, 2015, written at 9:45 a.m. Tristan first states the following, to his mom,

Just trust me, ride it out with me, Mom, this poetic endeavor, someone, something will happen or come of it. I know it.

Continued introduction to the poet Tristan Ray Thompson!

My name is Tristan Ray Thompson, I am thirty-seven years young, from Lexington, Kentucky, as I've stated before. I call my poetry esoteric poetry. Sometimes, for I speak often of high philosophy, theology, with hints at "mystic Christianity" and ancient symbolic philosophy, with a dash here and there of Kabbalistic, Rosicrucian, and Freemasonic symbolic philosophy.

I, the writer for Tristan, have no idea what most of what Tristan described in the above words is, but I do know a little bit about Tristan. He has been seeking knowledge through the philosophies of the world and through the Holy Word of God. The one thing I can say for sure about Tristan is this, I know that during his life journey here, he, at one time, gave his life to the Lord Jesus Christ. And at the end of his short life, he was once more reconciled to the Lord Jesus Christ as his Lord and Savior. And later, I will give you my reason for this statement, which I believe to be true.

Tristan continues his writings by saying the following,

> I pay my dues to Christ Jesus, through poetry by writing of Him, while inspired by the Holy Spirit. I also write "acronym poems."

The Lord spoke these words in Jeremiah 1:5,

> Before I formed you in the womb, I knew you.

In his supernatural brilliance, our great God is constantly having thoughts toward us, as individuals. Our great God knows all about us, and He wants us to know Him in all His glory.

Tristan continues by stating the following,

> Recently, even in my current exile, I heard a powerful speaker at a program I was attending, and the speaker said the following, "The most important thing in your life, is simply what you give thought to and about for most of your time…" (Michael Johnson)

Tristan continues with the following words,

> I submit to you no aphorism, therefore, but something freestyled right off the top of my head: Love is the highest aspect or quality known

to man, love is eternal, it is also selfless, and sacrificial, and every great poem or novel was written about and built upon by love in some form.

Isn't it refreshing to know that someone (God) has been the spiritual illumination in the lives of His children/ I rise! Amen!

Tristan Is My Name!

Many moons I might make mine, the lesser lunar light,
Yet will soon in me divine things, Mystic, Magic, Might,
Love and Truth, and Life, and Light/Teach me, Rabbi, please!
I will follow with delight and rest on prayerful knees,

[I the writer would like to state the following concerning Tristan's last line, I believe, the very best place for a human being to be is on his or her knees before the Lord.]

Fill my time with many moons, Oh Lord, and bless the night, forever more, I fear no evil, ever present light.
A servant unto you oh Lord, cruel I came,
But nonetheless, Poetic Prophet.
Tristan is my name!
(From the ashes I rise!)

This next writing from Tristan expounds on the following topic, how God can be self-existent! So let's hear what Tristan has to say about this topic.

Brief outlines of how I will expound on particular topics, this one is concerning the topic of how God can be self-existent, and using our limited comprehension. This is just an outline, a map, at many points in this teaching I may deviate from this and just free style speak.

> "How God can be self-existent!/Our limited comprehension!"
>
> How God can be self-existent! Good afternoon, my name is Tristan Ray Thompson, thank you for joining me. Let us pray, "Father in heaven, we humbly ask You to have mercy on us, sinners, we thank You for Your many blessings and Your promises. We ask that You bless this lecture, and all who hear this lecture, in Jesus mighty name. Amen!"

In the next teaching concerning Tristan's writings, we can see the following principle taught by the Lord and Savior, Jesus Christ. He was speaking to His disciples, commenting on how a certain incident came to be. He states that if they themselves have faith, not only would they be able to do the same thing our Lord did, but they would accomplish greater things than what they witnessed. This teaching is in reference to the fig tree parable! But I myself have what I consider a deeper meaning to this parable.

I believe that Jesus Christ, having taken on flesh, in order to fulfill the prophecies, naturally, as the writer has said, was intending to teach His disciples that they also would be empowered to do the signs and wonders our Lord did. But at the same time, for us not to use the gift of God for anything else, except to glorify God. We have this teaching in Hebrews 4:15. Let's hear the Word of God.

> For have we not an high priest which cannot be touched with the feeling of our infirmities, but was in all points tempted like as we are, yet without sin.

So we can learn from this that first, our Lord Jesus Christ was hungry and, naturally, after finding the fig tree barren, could have used His divine power to cause the fig tree to produce fruit, to cause fruit to appear. However, if the Lord Jesus Christ became flesh, in the flesh, He was tempted, but chose to express His divinity instead of His fleshly desires. Here, the enemy tries to cause us to serve self instead of the One True God.

So what does our Lord do? Hear these words—this is an awesome teaching. Check this out. This is brilliant. He not only refuses to use His divine power to satisfy His carnal physical being but also pronounces the fig tree should no longer bear fruit, forever. My thoughts on this teaching are as follows—this incident was a very powerful majestic demonstration of the Lord's loyalty and love for His Father's divine purpose, to fulfill His Father's will here upon the earth.

We can also see our Lord's steadfast refusal to deviate from any point upon the heavenly commission given to Him by the Father. This very same explanation applies to all the suffering the Lord Jesus endured before the crucifixion and during the crucifixion. As we look at the many miracles of our Lord and Savior Jesus Christ, they were performed for the benefit of others and for the glory of His Father in heaven.

> All the Lord's healings, His raising people from the dead, casting out demons, giving sight to the blind, causing the lame to walk—in all this, our Lord refused to use His divine power to benefit Himself, to use His power to relieve Himself of any physical sufferings to his flesh. Our Lord refused to alter the course the Father had set before Him. Only after every hint of physical pain had been endured, after He rises from the dead, then He wields His divine power and declares to His disciples upon seeing them. "It is I, do not be dismayed. Touch Me. Feel Me, and see." Like all that Our Lord has done, His teaching is of multitudes of meanings and are deep and profound. I, Tristan, no longer wonder at the awesomeness of this being mankind has chosen to call God. My question to myself is this, How come I can't keep my mind off of Him? And this, for the last twenty years. My friends, I'm smart enough to know that God is who He says He is.

Tristan Ray Thompson

A poem related to the "Reflections on
Scripture" by Tristan Ray Thompson

Can't get my mind off of you! (A love story about God).
From boy to man, from home to jail,
From a hundred different prison cells,
From 14 to 37 years old, and all the science I've been told,
From the peak of my sin, in an earthly hell,
From the bottom of a pit, in which I fell,
In the midst of my study of philosophies,
I can still hear your voice…calling me!
Forever I have felt your touch,
Even in my dreams.
I've run because it was too much for me,
A supernatural thing.
But no matter where I go,
Or what evil I do,
Why is it that I can't get my mind off of you?
(Now He speaks)
Jesus: I hear you, Tris, I'm near you Tris, and here's the reason why
I knew you before you were born, Tris,
My how the time does fly,
The answer to your question son,
Is in your question too!
For ever since the creation…
I can't get my mind off of You!

Tristan Ray Thompson
03-12-2015

A further comment by Tristan states the following:

> Writing this really shook me up tremendously. I even broke down intensely, and I feel as if I was talking to Him through this writing, using this poetic dialogue...

This next writing by Tristan is in reference to poetic reflections on scripture titled "And God said 'Let Us'" (Gen. 1:26).

>Through timeless tunnels travel three,
>Three they be... Are One indeed!
>The ethers fabric shudders: Blessed!
>For even molecules confess!
>Recondite to the wicked, This...
>And greet with only rancor kiss.
>Yet in vain, all opposition:
>Ephemeral disposition!
>Wherefore disdain will prophecy fulfill...
>Divine will!
>And order out of chaos manifests...
>Many blessed!
>Disconsolate eyes will rise to glimpse the skies,
>And will see...
>A mystery of one composed of three,
>Perfectly.
>Through the tunnels timeless we will travel,
>In the power.
>And by Him who slams the righteous gavel,
>At that hour...
>Will be told to us the mystery,
>Many be,
>Of which this one appears so beautifully,
>The Trinity!

This next writing by Tristan is, again, referring to reflections on scripture, this one titled "Pick a Side."

Tristan starts this writing off by stating the following:

> Look at how blind we have become! I speak about mankind as a collective whole because I too have demanded signs and wonders that would defy the laws of physics, in order that my faith might be strengthened. I won't say whether or not I received the signs and wonders I asked for, but if I did, they came at times when I didn't ask for them. At any rate, upon closer scrutiny, we discover how absurd, selfish, ungrateful, and elementary such a demand is…from our great God and creator.
>
> "The Miracle" the signs and wonders that we ask for are right here in front of us—it's ourselves. It is you, in your complete being, it is me, it is her, it's them, it's us, and we're standing in the miracle of God every day, breathing it in, and looking out at the night sky and seeing the glory of God displayed. If a person can't see the glory of God, just in his or her own being, the uniqueness of their own individuality, then indeed, we have become stubborn and hardhearted people.
>
> Wow! How did we become so calloused, so hardhearted to the voice of our Lord and become willingly blind to the Lord's truth? It's as if a veil has been drawn over our eyes and hearts. The apostle Paul specifically addresses this issue in the Lord's word found in the book of Romans 1:20. The Lord's word declares the following, "For the invisible things of Him from the creation of the world are clearly seen, being understood by the things that are made, even the eternal power and Godhead, so that they are without excuse."

This is such a brilliant expression concerning the concept of a living God. It is no great wonder that it is found in the Lord's Holy Word. I mean, to be alive in this amazing universe, here upon this earth, which I believe goes against all odds of mathematical probability, and to actually be aware that we are a conscience living soul or being...

Looking at all the wide variety of plant and animal life on this planet... And yet say to ourselves, I still demand a sign from the heavens above before I'll believe. Or is this just some random accident that has appeared out of confusion and chaos?

We insist that the Lord God would show us a sign... This, to me, is almost as ridiculous and recalcitrant as a man standing in the Kentucky River and saying, "Hell, Jimmy-Joe, I can't find any water in which to fish in, and yet this same man is soaked from his feet to his waist in the very waters he's standing in, which existence he stubbornly denies."

It may seem absurd, this water analogy, but we can see its truth. This is exactly the same as seeing the creation of God, yet denying its truth. When Jesus walked the earth, approximately two thousand years ago, He did many signs and wonders. So much so, that the book of John 21:25, declares the following words, "And there are also many other things which Jesus did, the which, if they should be written every one, I suppose that even the world itself could not contain the books that should be written, Amen."

And all that the Lord did was for our benefit, and for the honor and glory of God the Father. Most of mankind do not witness the signs and wonders of our mighty God, and I believe this is for the following reason. It's found in the book of Mark 6:5–6. Let's hear the Word of God, "And he [Jesus] could there do no mighty work save that He laid His hands upon a few sick folk and healed them, and He marveled because of their unbelief, and He went round about the villages teaching."

Also, our Lord declares the following in the book of Mark 16:17–18, "And these signs shall follow them that believe, in my name they shall cast out devils, they shall speak with new tongues, they shall take up serpents, and if they drink any deadly thing, it shall not hurt them, they shall lay their hands on the sick, and they shall recover." So if you desire to see signs and wonders, don't ask for your own selfish reasons, ask for the glory and honor of our great God, and simply believe.

The Lord spoke these words to Martha in the book of John 11:40. Let's hear the Word of God. "Jesus saith unto her, said I not unto thee if thou wouldest believe, thou shouldest see the glory of God, and henceforth called Lazarus from the dead after four days of being in a cave called a tomb."

Also in the book of John 20:29, the Lord's word declares the following, "Jesus saith unto him, Thomas because thou hast seen Me, thou hast believed, blessed are they that have not seen and yet believed."

Life is short, my friends. There are only two choices for man, serve self or serve God, pick a side, my friend. My prayer for you all is to choose wisely. Your very own life is your sign, your wonder, your miracle, and your evidence.

Your friend,
Tristan Ray Thompson
03-31-2015

ROBERT HERNANDEZ

The following poem follows this writing by Tristan.

The Poet's Pledge…the Power of Rhyme

A sign!
Requested I for a time of the Divine.
Amidst a world supernatural,
And mysteries sublime.
And when the ancient one gave me no sign,
To the earth I fell dismayed, and to the skies, I yelled.
This grave, this well of tired tears so grim, with sin,
Bemused, therein I swim.
By my darkness, light is dimmed,
Juxtaposed serenity accompanies my plight,
As my reflection in the well of tears becomes a light.
Reach in your hand!
Reach in oh Lord and save me from myself,
I can't fathom thine mysteries, alone and with no help.
At your feet, I surrender.
Teach this accomplished fool,
"Jesus speaks" Arise at once from your submersion,
In this wretched pool, look at thy reflection son,
Tell me what you see,
"I speak" only see I sadden eyes,
For what seems, will not be,
"Jesus speaks" Yet I see a miracle,
Yes in my image made.
"I speak" Wherein is the miracle in racing to the grave,
"Jesus speaks" the grave does not hold any power
over them that are deserving of life,
"I speak" Great and many are my sins…will faith alone suffice?
"Jesus speaks" Faith and works, now tarry
not, you have much work to do.
"I speak" Indeed I will then, let me start by writing poems for you.
A sign I requested for a time from the Divine, All the while,
I am the sign, I am the power of rhyme, the sign.

The divine art is not only represented in the incomprehensible mystery and beauty of the complete creation, but I believe it's also evident and very unmistakable to any person that is proficient in mathematical probability and statistics, as well as to the student of prophecy. There are over three hundred prophecies according to Tristan's understanding of the Lord's word, three hundred specific prophecies in the Old Testament about the coming of the Messiah Jesus Christ. Let's think about this for a minute, the next time you look at the last book in the Lord's Holy Word, the book of Revelation, and look at the words of our Lord and Savior Jesus Christ, as He declares the Word of God found in Hebrews 10:7.

> Then said I, Lo, I come [in the volume of the book it is written of me] to do thy will. O God.

Also in Psalms 40:7, we can hear these words from our Lord.

> Then said I, Lo, I come, in the volume of the book it is written of me.

It's almost exactly, the very same words found in the book of Hebrews. I write this to show how the Lord always confirms His word through scripture.

The renowned author Dr. James Gills, in his book titled, *Exceeding Gratitude for the Creator's Design*, Dr. Gills stated that he computed the odds of one man, the man Jesus Christ of Nazareth, fulfilling the more than three hundred—Old Testament prophecies about Himself. In the short period the Lord Jesus Christ walked the earth, by using the law of compound probability, to be astronomical, it's a number so large it would appear to be an impossibility.

Let's take for example the prophecy spoken by the prophet Isaiah in chapter 9:6–7. It goes as follows—there are five details in verse 6. Based on the law of compound probability, this comes out to be one chance in thirty-two, but if we take verses 6 and 7 together, which entails another five details, a total of ten details, which increase the odds to one in one thousand and twenty-four.

If we go to Isaiah 53:2–12, let's hear this prophecy written about eight hundred years before our Lord and Savior was born and walked the earth. This prophecy is considered by most as the prophecy that is commonly known as the passage known as the suffering servant. And there are thirty-two so-called fulfilled predictions within these passages, and the math behind this, based on the law of compound probability, for this one man, Jesus Christ, to fulfill every one of these predictions spoken of in these scriptures, is one in 4,294,967,296. That's right, over one in four billion plus.

The examples and prophecies go on and on. You can verify this information by using the *Dake's Annotated Reference Bible*, if you so choose to do so. Please understand that, with the law of compound probability, each detail of a prophecy doubles the chances of the prediction not being fulfilled.

A prophecy with just one detail has a one in two chance of coming to pass or being fulfilled. It will either be fulfilled or not. A prophecy with two details has a one in four chance of being fulfilled. Again for all you math teachers, I'm not talking about two prophecies. I'm talking about two details in one prophecy. When we talk about seven details in one prophecy, this has a one in 128 chance of being fulfilled.

So you see, my friends, apart from divine power, many of these, if not all of these, prophecies concerning the Lord Jesus Christ would not be fulfilled. And some of you might be thinking I'm on some religious trip! Yes, I may be on a trip, tripping off the math! I just wanted to share this with you, my friends, and all who read my poems, the brilliance of this mystery as I see it, especially to those of you who have an eye for "The Divine Art."

> Love:
> Tristan Ray Thompson
> 04-15-2015

This next writing by Tristan is titled "Spellbinding."

> To the center, a point of compass begins the design.
> He applies the square, next comes the great plumb line,
> Ex officio, the architect, the command is given.
>
> Drawn with wisdom, without hands, a circumscription
> In their craft, one as three, three as one, the triune God,
> Vexed is not, the mystery is as the sun, stars, and moon,
> Interspersed among the cosmic trail…clues so briefly,
> Notice on a starry night familiar spirit sweetly,
> Ever-shining, angelic delight, in moments fleeting,
>
> Arcane yet, not without light, hid from the deceiving.
> Retrospection of this retrospective, flaw not finding,
> The divine art, masterpiece, it's beauty so spellbinding.

Tristan goes on to say that of the Lord's beauty he does see, and of the Lord's truth he does see, he finds these daily in the Lord's creation. He further states that on the sword of the Lord he does not need any reminding.

The next writing by Tristan is titled "In the Name of Truth," reflections on scripture.

Tristan starts this teaching off by referring us to a scripture found in our Lord's word in Acts 26:24.

> Let's hear the Word of God. And as he thus spoke for himself, Festus said with a loud voice, Paul thou art beside thyself, much learning doth make thee mad.

This was the statement made to the ex-radical Pharisee named Saul of Tarsus, who later wrote at least half of the New Testament.

During his interrogation by King Agrippa, and by the governor Festus, this man who was formerly called Saul, but is now known by the name of Paul, had earlier in his life as a Pharisee who went about persecuting many who followed the teachings of the Lord Jesus Christ and tried his best to rid the Jewish community and nation of these so-called followers of Jesus Christ.

Paul, who at the time of the stoning of Stephen, the first Martyr of the Lord Jesus Christ, advocated the stoning of Stephen. According to the Word of God, as Saul was on the road to Damascus to further persecute the followers of Jesus Christ, he was struck down by a blinding light, and from out of the light came a voice saying, "Saul, Saul, why are you persecuting Me?"

And he said, "Who are you, Lord?"

Then the Lord said, "I am Jesus, whom you are persecuting."

The awesome thing about this encounter with the Lord Jesus Christ is Saul is struck blind. He needs to be led into the city of Damascus, where he prays and fasts for three days when he receives a visitor by the name of Ananias, who informs Saul he has been sent to lay his hands on Saul so he may receive his sight and be filled with the Holy Spirit. And the Lord also spoke these words regarding Saul, through the disciple Ananias.

> But the Lord said to him, "Go, for he is a chosen vessel of Mine to bear My name before Gentiles, kings, and the children of Israel. For I

will show him how many things he must suffer
for My name's sake."

Saul gives his life and service to the Lord Jesus Christ. Saul now becomes known as the apostle Paul, who goes about teaching and preaching Jesus Christ as Lord and Savior. He started many of the new churches. He performed many signs and wonders in the name of Jesus Christ, and he had a death before dishonor love for his Lord and Savior. His loyalty to the Lord Jesus Christ is beyond question. All who knew Paul at the end of his service to the Lord knew of his sincerity and dedication. Paul himself says in one scripture he has finished the race the Lord had set before him. In 2 Timothy 4:7, let's hear the word of the Lord.

I have fought the good fight, I have finished
my course, I have kept the faith.

As we go back to that day that Paul stood before king Agrippa and the governor Festus for his proclamation of the truth concerning Jesus Christ, they had thought Paul had lost his common sense, for they formerly knew him as a man of education, well-educated, a Pharisee, so much so, he was called a zealot for the sect of the Pharisees. And it amazed them that he now was an advocate for what was known as the way—those who followed the teachings of the Lord Jesus Christ.

It was hard for them to truly believe Paul was a true follower of the Lord Jesus Christ, knowing that, at one time, Paul once persecuted all those he could find who followed the way was now attempting to convince all those who hear his words to receive Jesus as Lord and Savior. Their only response to his words were the following—they attempted to explain his condition as one who no longer possessed a sane mind.

The question I've wonder at, is why? Why was it so hard for them to receive Paul's testimony concerning the Lord Jesus Christ? It's the same question I have for the majority of mankind today. Why? Why is it so hard for us to receive the testimony about Jesus Christ given to us through the Word of God?

Give this some serious thought. Out of the original twelve apostles, as the Lord Jesus Christ had as His followers, ten were martyred according to the writings of history. They have been called heroes of the faith, dedicated with soldier-like faith and loyalty. For the most part, they were tortured to death. But down through history, the numbers of those that have given their lives down through history for the Lord Jesus Christ is a number that only the Lord God knows.

Peter, according to history, was crucified upside down. John the Baptist was beheaded. Many were burned to death. And the list goes on and on.

Why did these people lay down their lives for the Lord Jesus Christ? I believe none of those that lost their lives for the Lord ever recanted or denied their Lord Jesus Christ. They remained loyal to their faith and their Lord and Savior. I also don't believe they received any mercy from their enemies, but I also believe they received strength from their Lord at the time of their need to endure their trials.

There are historians who have written about the followers of Jesus Christ and their loss of life for Jesus Christ in specific detail, such as Josephus, also Greek historians, and Jewish historians. And for the most part, these all agree or are compatible.

For what purpose would a man or woman endure such suffering? If not for what he or she has come to believe is absolutely true. What must a person see or hear that would convince them without a doubt to have such a strong conviction concerning the truth about Jesus Christ? For a person to stand up for his or her faith unto their death. Tristan believes that all these people simply received the truth of God's word—believed it and lived it out in their lives.

> Lee Strobel has written a few books concerning the Lord Jesus Christ, in one of his books titled *The Case for Christ*. Tristan believes that Strobel demonstrates brilliantly and vividly that there is more historical written proof for the deity of Jesus Christ, than there is against it. But we as people choose to believe a lie rather than the truth of God's word. We would rather exalt

ourselves than humble ourselves before our great and mighty God.

We've taken ourselves to a level where we believe that we're all-knowing, not only about our lives, but also, we become self-proclaimed experts on the subject of "God." We believe that we have authority concerning all things, even religious matters. Yet we haven't even taken the time to study the Holy Word of God. Why? Because we believe we are already enlightened to matters concerning the one true God, and this is done through a false light. Enough is enough. The truth is that I am a sinner, simply saved by grace through faith in the Lord Jesus Christ.

My name is Tristan Ray Thompson, and I am a sinner, called a saint by the grace of God, through the gift of faith given to me by the Holy Spirit. I'm no pastor or preacher, but I do see the light, for His glory and honor. He has allowed me to see the truth, now today as well as the years ago. And with these words and poems I write, I want to shine the light upon you. In the name of truth.

Tristan Ray Thompson
04-07-2015

This next poem written by Tristan.

In Truth's Name

In the name of truth and love, with providence sublime,
Nails and whips and death became the cup of the Divine.
Trumpets did announce His bold approach to Calvary,
Reverential angels sense the coming victory,
Understanding that some would not appreciate…

Triumphed He above the sorrow…did not hesitate,
Here-to-fore it was proclaimed of old and came to be,
Stalwart in the name of Truth, He came for you and me.

Near the throne, the trumpets crack the sky, and angel's fly,
At the same time, Satan will cause many to deny,
Many will still be declaring, show us signs and proofs,
Even with the trumpets blaring in the name of Truth.
Diligently, prayerfully, written this day, at 9:30 a.m., 04-07-2015.

>Tristan Ray Thompson
>(A spark from the divine flame)
>In His Honor

Tristan adds this at the end of this poem,

>Mom, I really put my heart and soul into this one, and made no mistakes, corrections, or substitutions. It is under these circumstances (when it just flows from my pen) that I feel divinely inspired. (If I may be so bold.)

This next writing by Tristan is short, but I believe it is very powerful. There's no title, but here's his writing.

>Adam walks off with the gift of free will, and God says to Himself, "It's time, Jesus embraced by the unity of God the Father, and God the Holy Spirit, looks down upon Adam who is about to commit the first sin and declares, with a tear in His eye, don't worry, I'm coming. I knew that this was going to happen, and my love for you is greater than your sin."

>By: Tristan Ray Thompson
>04-07-2015

This next writing of Tristan's is once again titled "Reflections on Scripture/Free will and accountability (Why bad things happen)." It's based on the Word of God found in Proverbs 3:5. Let's hear the Word of God. The Word of God declares, "Trust in the Lord with all your heart, and lean not on your own understanding."

This argument is nothing new to mankind. We've asked ourselves this question many times. Our own personal philosophy though is a vast combination of esoterica, mystic mathematical assumptions, and of course, the Holy Bible. My preoccupation with quantum theory. The universe and the one true God has led me to some very definite conclusions, which I will not be sharing at this time.

I desire to have this subject or topic to be reserved for a video lecture that I hope to produce sometime in early 2016. I feel that it would only compromise the integrity of both the subject and my discourse on it, to try to sum it up completely here, so I shall do so briefly herein.

Suffice it to say, however, the fabric of reality, as "we" perceive it and experience it is really collectively subjective and only gives the illusion of objective uniformity. The top quantum physicians of today observe that a "wave" or "particle" only begins to behave like it is one or the other, upon being observed by the observer. This isn't even the wild part. I plan to talk about this in the video I plan to make concerning this subject.

Free will and accountability plays into all of life on a much grander scale. I'll do my best to illustrate this to you the reader, through these next words.

Let's take for example that we have a person that we'll call A, and A is driving drunk and runs over a person we'll call B. And person B is an eight-year-old little girl. Some people in our world would place the blame on God. They also would blame person A. And they would demand to know where was God in this incident and what God was doing during this incident. Now let's interject a person we'll call C who happens to be a Christian woman who is a grandmother. And this person just happens to die of lung cancer, despite having the Christian community praying for her.

Some will question or doubt the true existence of God. But this holographic universe, created by God, is to maintain certain balances that are based on free will. For example, person A, the drunk driver, cannot be held accountable for his actions, or understand the implications of his actions, if person B, who is the little girl, is miraculously saved by the grace of the living God. Then anyone could drive drunk because there are no consequences for driving drunk. No one we'll hold them accountable for their actions or for what happens or could happen because of their drunk driving. And if person C is miraculously healed from her lung cancer, after smoking for more than fifty years, then she also has not been held accountable for her actions, which she chose through her free will.

In other more unique situations, a much bigger picture must be considered. Of which, I hope to discuss in the coming year of 2016. A much broader philosophy, such as esoteric, math, and situational soul ejection. For now, I leave you with the words written by King Solomon, found in Proverbs 3:5

Trust in the Lord with all your heart, and lean not on your own understanding.

> Love your friend, Kentucky's own, Tristan Ray Thompson.
> (Situational soul ejection is a term I created for one of my own theories.)
> 04-16-2015

This next writing by Tristan is what I, the writer, consider very unique. I myself have not seen poetry in this manner. But let me share Tristan's writing. It starts off in this manner,

> Hello, Mom, my best and sweetest friend, and biggest fan!

I'd like to interject, at this time, my perspective on these words from the following poem. I know how true these words are that have been written by Tristan. I myself have witnessed this truth firsthand, lived out both in Tristan's life and my life and in his mom's life. Let me continue with Tristan's writing.

He says he has evolved into a new level of poetic, supremely, he states.

> I went into my own form of prayer and meditation to produce this, what I call a masterpiece. I'd like for you to notice how difficult this form of poetry truly is. I believe that this is a poetic feat I accomplished through the gifts I have received from the one true God. And, Mom, please post it and really share this with the world. This style of poetry is not only acoustic, but since I used the acoustic form on both the beginning and the ending of this poem, it's something even more unique. I don't know what to call it. Double acoustic? Google it for me and see what it might be called. Now this poem is called "The Romance of Tristan and the King."

To do thy will Lord I submiT
Redeem me, this shameful sinneR
In thy presence, anxious am I
Shaken, nervous: oh my sinS
Touch me, fill my heart with lighT
As I behold…thine enigmA
Never could I ignore the soN
(and never can this love be undone)
And now the King responds…
To the King, you bow, in Me you trusT
Having My knowledge, and faith made througH
Evermore I submit, to the one God who is truE
King of all Kings, your face I will always seeK
In thy presence…humble am I
Nevermore shame…evermore forgiveN
Great my airborne spirit, to be with my KinG
(To my delight, for thou art risen!)

Most Sincerely:
Tristan Ray Thompson

 This is the one, a sublime work, what I believe is a wonderful literary accomplishment. Enjoy! Be thou entertained!
 Note: Mom, I picked this up later in the day, at least several times and read it aloud to myself and experienced that familiar static electricity…you know, when the hairs on your arms stand up! This poem, for me, actually "reads" like a kind of—I don't really know how to say it correctly—like it's magical or something.
 I know He is with me. Sometimes, I believe it's the Holy Spirit working through me because, at those times, it just flows from my pen. There is something weird about me, Mom, I think, or believe I have a gift. I told Beto once that I

wanted to be in the healing ministry because of this intense experience. I need to do something with it. I love you, Mom!

This next poem written by Tristan is titled "The Sound of Light."

> Luminus and without…ebB
> Effulgence…untamablE
> Torch of truth dispel the night
> with Glory uncontainable!
> Triune Lord which worketh spelL
> Hearts like mine fell under did I
> Entertained by ethereal…sonG
> Ringing in my ears…I sigH
> Ever plays upon my sighT
> "The Sound of Light"

"From the author"
Tristan Ray Thompson

I wrote this to illustrate a spiritual experience, for which normal or everyday lexicon is inadequate to successfully describe this spiritual experience. For example, symbols are used to express concepts that transcend easy verbal explanation. But here is my poetry. There is no room or place for symbols, therefore, I have to speak symbolically! A symbolic expression, for instance, is the implication that "light" can be heard. Such a suggestion is immediately received as incongruous with terrestrial experience. However, since I speak of celestial experiences, I use this type of verbal symbolism. I believe that it should not sense to the carnal mind, which is what I consider to be those who live in this world according to the principles found in the Holy Word of God. To all who read and enjoy my writings, welcome to my world and my craft of esoteric poetry!

Love In Christ:
Tristan Ray Thompson
04-28-2015

The poem below is another poem written by Tristan.

Ye Old Art

Twinkle in the night sky…cosmic eyes,
Silent, speaking…softly spoken,
Endless, timeless…far beyond,
Cast about, this supernatural power!
I stare into Oh, the hand that the night sky,
Supernatural dust,
Silver glitter has transfixed me,
Oh, the hand that owns this supernatural,
Prepare I, to search for thee!
Journey through the night sky, astral flight,
Flight of soul…accomplish I,
The body safe and sound asleep,
I breathe, don't weep, I breathe, tis sleep.
At one with the night sky,
How fly I?
This art that no one taught to me,
Nature's hidden mystery,
Glimpse into the night sky,
Yearn to fly!
"A spark from the divine flame"

By: Tristan Ray Thompson
07-16-2015

THE MIRACLE OF TRISTAN RAY THOMPSON

The following are short writings by Tristan:

Concreteness of an Abstract

Thoughts, like stains, indeed remain, thoughts…
In the air they hang, where they were born,
Follow me on the wings of a poem… In a dream,
Where a scene awaits…forlorn.

A Cell

'Twas a disorderly arrangement I,
Beheld spellbound!
Thoughts cast about, ceiling wall and ground.
Some, cringing in a corner…abject and abandoned,
Others, indifferent to where and how they landed,
In the center there… Look! A thought like a book,
See how it glows, how it towers sublimely!
And by the window there… Look! sneaking like a crook,
Half in/half out…as if to say.

A Crime

This crowded cave of homeless thoughts,
That welcome the distraught,
How many years are you here?
How many born of tears?
Old thoughts, young thoughts, sad thoughts and mad,
Remorseful thoughts, and some plain bad, none glad,
And the people will come and go,
But never will the vernal bloom,
Occur in this concrete tomb,
For certain is the gloom for the thoughts
in the room.
Forever in prison…their doom.

ROBERT HERNANDEZ

Thoughts!
"A spark from the divine flame"
07-20-2015

This next writing by Tristan is titled "The Power of Words."

"The Power of Words"

A poet dreamed a dream, a most disturbing thing,
On the wings of a poem, let us flee into the scene, follow me,
'Twas a confused war zone to behold, weapons told,
Words were arrows shot cold, to and fro,
Bone and marrow both pierced most fierce,
I saw power bold inside the word unfold,
For as a poet, this a most striking moment,
In the evolution of my conscientiousness
The spoken word, an oxymoron personified,
For long both tangible and intangible,
You can't grab it and hold it…yet,
You can feel it and it can grab you.
So I then took the oath…the oath of poetic office!
Three whom I have yet to see, never grant me be,
So hopeless in my recourse,
To thoughtful words neglect,
So ardent in my passion,
To harmful words then fusion,
Uncircumspect,
For I recant the error I,
Have in my fever folly wrought,
Self-produced! Poet king I be,
While self-taught, also,
Can by my own words be,
Brought to naught.
"Words"

THE MIRACLE OF TRISTAN RAY THOMPSON

So shall the poet sternly shun the profane
As diamonds glisten, I am Tristan,
"A spark from the divine flame"
07-25-2015

This next writing by Tristan is titled

The Interrogation of Cupid

Wilt thou aim at one, not two?
Tell me, thou with arrows flying.
For it is because of you,
A Virgo knight hath done much crying,
Yet I long for that first sting,
Where the heart does flitter high,
When it seems the stars did sing,
And frequent came those butterflies,
The only time I walked on air,
And magic forest was my home,
Is when I had but just one care,
And though in company…alone.
A poet king, naturally, thou be struck,
A romantic, under Virgo's sign,
Of all thine targets! Just my luck!
Could thou not another find?
Tell me, ye whom blindly shoots,
Bewitched arrows carelessly,
What have I to do with you?
When have I conversed with you?

A story from the "Table Round,"
Unto which ye must have listened,
Though it was in days and knights,
Thou has mistook me for Tristan,
Anathema be upon thee,
Thou oh Cupid, born of Greece,

> For by your be-damned arrows,
> Romantic souls will find no peace.

Note from the author, Tristan Ray Thompson:

Such romantic tragedies are far too typical when the Lord Jesus Christ is not involved. This poem reflects not only my own, but I believe it applies to many people's collective experiences. Too often, we are guided into the illusion of love, for if Christ isn't involved, and both parties do not have a real and true relationship with the living God through faith in Jesus Christ, the relationship will more than likely fail. The late Jimi Hendrix is quoted as saying, "Even castles in the sand drift into the sea eventually."

And so I think to myself that when we build anything without the involvement of the Lord, we might as well be building upon the shifting sands of our own wisdom. I don't know if ole Jimi had that thought in his mind when he spoke those words, but it fits.

The Lord Jesus does, however, speak of such an analogy. It's found Matthew 7:24–27. Let's hear the word of the Lord. "Therefore whoever hears these sayings of Mine, and does them, I will liken him to a wise man who built his house on the rock: and the rain descended, the floods came, and the winds blew and beat on that house, and it did not fall, for it was founded on the rock. But everyone who hears these words of Mine, and does not do them, will be like a foolish man who built his house on the sand, and the rain descended, the floods came, and the winds blew and beat on that house, and it fell. And great was its fall."

Lastly, Cupid represents the false, worldly, and pagan symbolic philosophy/theology, which is so utterly ridiculous. I use him in the poem because I believe that it's just as utterly ridiculous and prone to failure for us to pursue love without Jesus Christ, who is love, love eternal. God bless you all.
A spark from the Divine Flame!
05-18-2015

This next writing by Tristan is titled "Into the Mystery." Tristan states here that for some who read and have read his poems it's hard for us to receive the proper interpretation from his perspective, but he trusts in the Lord to bless those with the ability to come to understand and be enlightened by them.

Into the Mystery

Ninety-three million miles from the sun,
I'm born,
This strange place…this strange land,
With unthinking hands.
The burden of a man, and betwixt two…
Powers I'm torn…to the light sworn,
In a race against time,
to unite with "I AM"
Twenty-three point five-degree inclination,
The axis of my home,
As I journey around the sun,
Winter, Spring, Summer, Fall,
Into the Mystery…was my initiation,
Alone…
A memory from the past…a faint call,
Be.
Read.
Know.

Teach.
Heal.
Pray.
Preach.
Ninety-three million miles…yet not out of reach,
Born into the Mystery!

This next writing by Tristan is titled

"Ego" versus "I Am Awareness" (The Fading of the Illusion)

Ego: Me, mine, I, me, mine, I…I like me, mine, I…
I AM: What?
Ego: Oh, just singing my favorite song…me, mine, I…
I AM: Good Lord, do you ever shut up?
Ego: I want this, I want that, I am this, I am that,
I AM: You are not, in fact, I AM, and need not you…
Ego: Bull crap, you can't live without me, we are one.
I AM: Ah-Ha,! I got you…you said "we"
Ego: Ah-Ha! Got you… You said "You", as if to imply that I am a separate entity in the context of also being such a one to reckon with. Ha! I AM!
I AM: "Am not"…understand you are the illusion and every time I become aware of you…or…the symptoms of you rather, you become weaker, and I…stronger.
Ego: Don't say that, I mean don't think that!
I AM: I will, I will, I will, I AM.
Ego: Seriously, please stop, my survival depends upon it.
I AM: You have only hindered my progress, I must dissolve you, you are an imposter, and a phantom and your incessant ramblings have frustrated Me.
Ego: I don't want to go, how will I exist without form?
I AM: It's not always about you, you really are selfish.
Ego: But I'm scared to go.
I AM: It's OK, Don't be scared, this whole thing is foolish.

Ego: Why is it foolish?
I AM: Because in truth, you never were!

"I Am Awareness" is a term used in modern psychoanalytical theory to distinguish the true self from the nonself (ego).
A Spark from the Divine Flame
07-27-2015

This next writing by Tristan is titled "A Religious Post."

Upon many lengthy discussions with what I call self-proclaimed authorities, as well as they themselves, seem to think of themselves, on religious matters, who, mind you, have not heeded the apostle Paul's great advice, which is found in 2 Timothy 2:15, which teaches the following: "Study to show thyself approved unto God, a workman that needeth not to be ashamed, rightly dividing the word of truth."

I have met with a great mystery, how is this—rather…how is it that when a person comes to jail or prison, they somehow miraculously transform into authorities on just about every subject matter under the heavens? I, myself, had a cold the other day, or maybe it was a seventy-two-hour virus that I might have had, and lo and behold, as soon as I let it be known, everybody instantly transformed into doctors! You would have thought they had all graduated from Harvard Medical University, as if we all weren't in a federal prison.

I mean for all the…well, uh, you know, "What you need to do is, uh, drink plenty of liquids, and blah, blah, blah."

I'm like, "OK, thank you very much, Dr. Drug Dealer, Dr. Bank Robber." Preposterous, I say!

But my point is that this phenomenon of "quote-unquote," a magical profession of transformation, spills over into the topic of religion. These instant priests and theologians, and here goes all these instant priests, theologians, and atheist scientist, who I'm mainly addressing, self-proclaimed experts on religion who, for their foundation, stand on atheistic principles, though they probably couldn't spell it to save their lives.

So here they go, "Oh yeah, see, you know that Jesus really didn't do that or that, or that because of blah, blah, blah, blah."

Again, I say, "OK. Thanks for your input, Professor Crack Dealer."

It is frustrating. How can anyone learn anything when they already know everything?

I won't push my views on you, my readers, or put dogmatic spins on already existing truths. But as your friend who loves you, you know who you are...all of you, I challenge you to keep an open mind and do not let the distractors of today lull you into complacency and disinterestedness. Choose carefully for yourselves teachers whom you would learn from. And lastly, study to show thy own self-approved.

Peace and love to you in Jesus Christ.
Tristan Ray Thompson

This next writing by Tristan is titled "A Glimpse into the Mystery of Christ." Introduction to the follow-up is on the following page, "I Am That I Am."

A Glimpse into the Mystery of Christ

The puzzle my wit grasps in faith,
The mystery which long endures,
Endearing in its solemn call,
Beckoning with wordless ardor.
Manifesting everywhere I turn.
Study, learn, learn, learn…wisdom must be earned.
2,000 years of hectic tears, could not the flame unburn.
My doubts and fears, these abstract spears pierce,
Not for still yearn.
And travel in an astral trance,
Behold the frozen dance…
That height to which the birds aspire,
You can go no higher,
Drawn into the mystery,
Where math, magic, science, and light,
Illustrate the Lord Jesus Christ.
Follow me on the wings of a poem,
Let us flee,
With,
Words,
I've,
Prepared,
A,
Scene…follow me,
The decision made…the ethereal veil kissed.
Proclamation, conception, incarnation,
The mission realized, accepted.
Fire and water, air and earth, the star of David actualized.
The seal of Solomon personified.
The two…interlaced triangles concerning the cross,
Lo, I come…in the volume of the book, it
is written of me (Psalms 40:7).
Lion from the tribe of Judah,
Hundreds of prophecies fulfilled side by side,

The moment, the betrayal pre-determined, the suffering servant,
The crux of the matter.
The supernatural darkening of the sky…angels fly (Matt. 27:45),
Roman soldiers ponder events odd…this was God (Matt. 27:54).
Transcension and ascension, Holy Spirit manifest,
His words I will quote for you, the wise in this invest;
I am the door….(John 10:7)
All that ever came before Me, were thieves and robbers (John 10:8).
Before Abraham was…I AM (John 8:58).
I am not of this world…(John 8:24)
I am the way, the truth, and the life…(John 14:6)
I am the Alpha and the Omega, the beginning and
the end, the first and the last…(Rev. 22:13)
Except you see signs and wonders, ye will not believe…(John 4:48)
Lo, I come…in the volume of the book it
is written of Me (Psalms 40:7).

I Am That I Am
(End will not lose, [Exo. 3:14])

The wise invest, and will not lose,
Study to show thyself approved.
Math, magic, science, light…
Glimpse the mystery of Christ!

A spark from the divine flame
Tristan Ray Thompson

This next writing by Tristan is titled "The Oath"

The Oath

Proudly do I solemnly swear,
On this pen and on my hair,
Evermore to use this gift,

To edify, heal, and uplift,
Strive I will, too touch the heart,

Omit light, repel the dark,
Amplify the divine truths,
This is what I'm sworn to do.
Happily, with honor, I…rhyme to the KING…justified.
Until the end of time, it be… Mystery in my poetry!

03-31-2015

Note to the World!

I am the greatest, hands down,
I never stop. I dream in rhyme!
I'll never run out of rhymes,
or creating ways of writing them.
I am the best.
God on my side!
Look! See!

As the writer of Tristan's biography, concerning his writings, it may appear as if Tristan is exhibiting pride here with these last that he wrote. I believe it may contain a bit of pride on his part. But I also believe he knew who he was in Jesus Christ. He also knew that his gifts came from Jesus Christ. Knowing Tristan as I did, he truly was a gifted child as well as a child of God, the son of the King of Kings, and Lord of Lords!

This next writing by Tristan is titled "A Theatrical Presentation, Presented in Poetic Dialogue."

A Theatrical Presentation, Presented in Poetic Dialogue

Scene/setting: The dialogue begins just, "post crux." The accomplished chemist, ever ego fixated, is mocking the creator, God, after he discovers the potential to manufacture simple life forms in his laboratory.

The Lord manipulates the time-space continuum and manifests Himself in the laboratory, as a chemist, and confronts this proud chemist, at first as a fellow chemist, then as the living one true God.

In response, the Lord God's intervention is a result of both the self-inflated arrogance and pompous boastings of the chemist, and the unchanging desperate love God has for him. The combination of extreme opposites forces action.

THE CHEMIST: Alas, It's done! The fruit of my toil,
Needeth not sunshine, rain, nor soil.
The chemical marriage hath revealed my lot,
An elemental dance, merry magical motion,
A little bit of chance, and a sprinkle of a portion.
Immortalized in science books…I shall inherit!
For what I have created is a crown on my merit!
GOD: What is this you have done, young sir?
CHEMIST: I have dethroned God!
GOD: Shameful, is this thing you infer!
CHEMIST: Why does it strike you odd?
GOD: Let Me start over…do you know who I Am?
CHEMIST: No…do you work down the hall?
GOD: Not down the hall, not down the street, not around here at all.
CHEMIST: Well, how did you get in here.
GOD: Easy…I have the keys.
CHEMIST: There is only one set.
GOD: And those, belonging to Me!
CHEMIST: Enough of this rhetoric, tell me your name!

GOD: Suffice it to say, out of love, I came.
CHEMIST: I no longer need you, I will not listen.
GOD: However, your found in a precarious position,
for indeed you've used all the things that I have made.
To equal yourself to the Ancient of days.
Now ponder ye this, Oh proud chemist,
While standing upon your false premise,
In that, you have made something from something,
Make for Me now, young sir, something out of nothing!
The chemist pauses... Looks around his laboratory...
CHEMIST: Well...I, uh...
GOD: Well...You...Uh...What?
Chemist: I have to have something to start with,
God: Exactly, that's why your you, and I am Me, or We,
CHEMIST: Did you say your "We"?
GOD: Never mind, tell Me now, do you see your error?
CHEMIST: I uh...I apologize...what are You going to do to me?
GOD: Lots of love, nothing else, love you, forgive you,
over and over again, protect you, love you more, forgive you again
Forgive you, again and again, correct you, discipline you,
Love you, on and on and on...get it?
CHEMIST: That's wild, but why me, why so much love?
GOD: I created you, and mind you, from nothing!
GOD: What time do you have?

The chemist nervously looks behind him at the
    clock
without reasoning within himself that,
God already knows what time it is.
CHEMIST: It's a half past... Hey! Where did You
    go?
The Lord dematerializes, leaving the chemist
    alone in his laboratory,
he splashes water on his face, thinking that the
    long hours,
and lack of sleep has caused him
to daydream this whole experience, to imagine
    it all!
CHEMIST: Wow, what a dream, to create some-
    thing from nothing,
Impossible!
He leaves the laboratory, pondering,
walking down the hall he passes a professor...
A professor of astronomy.
PROFESSOR: Somebody was looking for you
    earlier.
CHEMIST: Who...why?
PROFESSOR: Some carpenter...
He said He had some work for you to do in the
    lab.
CHEMIST: You didn't ask Him His name?
PROFESSOR: Didn't think to ask Him...
I had just awakened from the wildest dream.
CHEMIST: Do tell!
PROFESSOR: I saw the solar system and the Milky
    Way,
and the entire universe go back in time,
In reverse...like at light speed...
Even to the singularity preceding the big bang,
And then there was nothing,
But conscientiousness, my conscientiousness,

and I heard some voices talking,
Three different beings, but They had the same voice,
just then, in the stillness, They spoke the word, "Be,"
And Boom!
What we as humans call the big bang, happened,
And everything else, the formation of the universe occurred.
PROFESSOR: Can you imagine, creation from nothing?

This next writing by Tristan is titled "The poetic Effusions...... Tourette's Suppression!"

The Poetic Effusions… Tourette's Suppression!

Atom-splitting equivalent, creativity, super-star explosions!
Neurons mega storm my mind…I am Tristan!
Tourette Syndrome Suppression…tics become frozen,
From this matrix, I've learned to tap into the wisdom!
Control the storm.
Electricity…shaped into a form!
Carve I jewels from ugly stones,
Power…I alone!
I place my foot upon the dragon's head,
Mercurius Trismegistus,
Order out of chaos, such a task!
Yet it can be done!
Could a criminal be given a crown?
Can the world understand the dilemma?
Can a throne and a home for a King be found?
Why fore this foreign cinema?
Wherefore come this…these maddening talents?
With which seek I to make known,

The life and mind of a Tourette syndrome sufferer,
Is both, at once…Amazing…and alone.

11-02-2015

  This next writing by Tristan is in reference to Tristan's dad, Tommy Thompson. It's titled: "'Twas an Honor to Call Him Dad!"
  Before I, the writer, begin this writing of Tristan's, I'd like to share some insights I've received from Tristan's mom concerning the relationship between Tristan and his dad. According to Tristan's mom, Angie, to start off, I believe it's safe to say that in almost every relationship, there is going to be good and bad. From what I understand, for the most part, is that the relationship Tristan had with his dad wasn't at its best during Tristan's later years. I can't express Tristan's feelings during his dad's last days, but I do know he loved his dad very much. And I base this opinion on the following poem Tristan wrote concerning his dad.

> I saw temperance and fortitude,
> I heard wise words and pragmatic discourse,
> I discerned a strong firm self-discipline,
> I felt a loving, sincere embrace, and beheld,
> A familiar friendly face,
> For thirty-five years…
> A great man I had the honor to know,
> Upon me this grace bestowed.
> I consider the idea, that had I not been born his son,
> I would not have been allowed in his house!
> The Lord indeed has a sense of humor,
> The man indeed did not deserve such a bad son,
> And I, I didn't deserve such a good father,
> Yet, there we were.
>
> In his last days…hours even, of his life,
> I held his hand,
> My mother, Angie heard me say to him,

THE MIRACLE OF TRISTAN RAY THOMPSON

Dad, I just want you to know you were a great father,
And he modestly replied I hope so Tris,
Through it all, with my uncle Rick watching,
I held on to his hand as he literally drew his last breath,
So peacefully....
It was as if an angel passed over him,
Swooped down, and took him home.
I hope he knew, how much I truly loved him.

A spark from the divine flame!
11-14-2015

This next writing by Tristan is titled "Confessions of the Wind."

Confessions of the Wind

Of the eternal, I am formed,
Beyond measure,
Concern thyself not to reckon.
I gently comb the hair of fields,
Sway grain's gold treasure,
Sweet eyes I beckon.
I cause the dance of leaves on trees,
And the soft song solemn sung.
In spring's ceremony, the supernatural scents with me,
Will warm a cold heart, like the Son.
I carry the word, and the memory bright,
Of the divine formation!
When love personified said;
Let there be light,
From this was my creation,
Evermore I travel!

A spark from the divine flame!
11-16-2015

ROBERT HERNANDEZ

This next writing by Tristan is titled "Void Abundance."

Void Abundance
(The Solitary Pricelessness of Love)

In the world of endless things,
The eyes are never full,
The ears struggle and strain,
To hear the words of fools,
And when your hands reach out to touch,
Those treasures worth so much,
A desperate clutch only finds dust,
Or fool's gold clothed in rust!
In a world of senseless things,
A man must prudent be,
A man must heed to heart, not mind,
And proceed carefully,
For love has many emotions,
Find it not in lust,
Romantic souls feel pain untold,
When gold crumbles to dust.
In this world of many things,
Must let the Spirit teach,
Much less the pain.
If you'll refrain,
From vain things within reach,
Many things are manifest,
Yet sent not from above,
So hear a rhyme,
That's worth your time,
The greatest find is love.

A spark from the divine flame!
11-17-2015

This next writing by Tristan is titled "A Theatrical Poetic Dialogue: God and the Prosecuting Attorney."

A Theatrical Poetic Dialogue
God and the Prosecuting Attorney

Scene/Setting: The poetic dialogue begins in the prosecutor's office, just minutes after a court session where a man has just been sentenced to the death penalty, for crimes of unspeakable evil. The prosecutor begins to contemplate Atheism, he cannot understand why God would allow so much suffering in the world, so much evil to continue and exist in this world. In his desperate and confused anger, he curses God. In God's merciful, sympathetic love, He uses a seldom practiced recourse, divine manipulation of the time-space continuum.

The conversation begins in the following manner, a knock on the prosecutor's door.

PROSECUTOR: Come in…I said come in…Whoa! [surprised]

GOD: Hey there [appears as a young modern carpenter, boots, tool belt, etc.]

PROSECUTOR: I didn't even hear you open or close the door.

GOD: I didn't use the door! Sometimes I forget, it gets old at times!

PROSECUTOR: Who are You…uh…how may I help You?

GOD: I am God, straight up, we're going to skip all the rhetoric today.

PROSECUTOR: Yeah right, get your crazy ass out of here,
or I'll call the police.

GOD: Mind if I smoke? [Turns into a cloud of smoke and hovers.]

PROSECUTOR: Holy Crap! [awe-stricken]

GOD: That's strike two potty-mouth! [God reappears as an old man.]

PROSECUTOR: Oh my God!

GOD: Yes? I'm listening!

PROSECUTOR: I mean…Jesus Christ! [shocked]

GOD: Silence! Now stand up straight, like a man. I'm going to explain this, in the best way I can. Who do you think you are…to question Me, God? You're not righteous by far…for I have seen you and known you, before the foundations of the world. And before you begin to contemplate My motives young man, first put your own affairs in proper order, if you can! For to be judged…by you, My own creation…is a preposterous, ridiculous insinuation.

PROSECUTOR: Please forgive me…I…I'm sorry, [God interrupts abruptly]

GOD: Done! Forgiven! Forgotten! I love you!

GOD: Mind if I smoke? [disappears again]

[A knock on the door awakes the prosecutor from a nap.]

JANITOR: Excuse me, sir….it's 9:00 p.m….you must have fallen asleep.

PROSECUTOR: Whew! My God, I mean my goodness, what a dream.

JANITOR: Have you been smoking in here, sir? It's a bit smoky in here.

A side note from Tristan to his mom.

    I think that I'm going to do a whole lot of these theatricals. You can do with it what you want. But you already know that I'd like this stored in my Facebook file. In this way, when I have the time to type it all up, I'll have it available. I wish I could actually direct a play like Shakespeare did. I've often given it much thought. My mind seems to function in this type of fashion. I can envision it all, how I would like to see it go. Oh well!
    Love you, Mom!

This next writing by Tristan is titled "For Power to a Son."

For Power to a Son"

Sky-born mystic, super-enigma,
I have arrived…
1977…The journey I barely survived!
I AM HERE! Lend an ear and a well-opened mind,
I can and will teach the mystery Divine,
Sandblast my flesh Lord,
The test I have taken,
Quick-fast…the one sword,
My spirit awaken,
Chastise my flesh now,
And reveal my purpose,
For only through deep pain,
will, power surface.

The following writing by Tristan is titled "The Wise Path."

ROBERT HERNANDEZ

The Wise Path

May I be spared recompense, for my recalcitrance,
For I foolishly thought I was wise!
Behind my cell door, many nights I've cried.
Hid from my friends, these teary Hazel eyes!
This temple illustrated by tattoos, I now despise,
In the height of my foolishness,
I thought myself so wise,
Behind an ink shield, a gentle soul revealed,
Heretofore, the lies of Lucifer adorned…
Decorated, I, in the carnal illusion.
Deserving of the grave, and immersed in confusion,
Lonely is the fool who thinks himself wise.
But in the depth of my folly, such a king,
A king with no crown, and a permanent frown,
Tis truly a heartbreaking thing.
I will admit my foolishness, O Lord,
Before Thee, I solemnly bow,
I pray, give me wisdom, for that I do thirst,
Forever your servant, I vow.
And if You do bless me, and dress me in light,
Send me to dry teary eyes,
I'll spend my days, pointing the way,
For fools to truly become wise.

04-16-2015

The following writing done by Tristan is titled "My Lord."

My Lord

In this battle I've engaged, how could I have not known?
That in the skies, a war is waged, before thy mighty throne,
I'm resolute, firm in resolve,
To watch, will not suffice.

Destitute and doomed to fall, Thine enemies I strike,
Thy word my only weapon true, for carnal, is not the fight,
Thy word as a melody of flutes and harps…the battle cry,
I touch the sky in meditation,
Into the front lines,
No fear, no doubt, or hesitation, mighty strength Divine!
I AM!
Mighty strength Divine I AM,
Christ in ME are We,
Through Him do all things, I can,
Behold the mystery.
For sins and tattoos…me they judge,
And truth appears as lies.
But God has chosen the foolish things of the world,
To now confound the wise.

Here I am Lord, send me!

02-28-2015

This next writing by Tristan is titled "A Creative Writing with a Dash of Poetry."

A Creative Writing with a Dash of Poetry

It is said by a particular tribe of descendants from the Aztecs,
That when a person dies, they merely wake up from a dream,
A dream that they were living,
Along with some other ridiculous absurdities,
Even more ludicrous on the other side of the globe.
Is the theory of…nothing!
Nothingness, oh, just plain and simple nothingness!
This theory puts me in mind of a person,
Who begins an attempt to formulate a hypothesis,
Then sets his pencil down and says…oh screw it.
As his intellectual integrity disintegrates,

At the approach of the devil's footsteps.
But do you want to know what the prisoner poet says?
Shall I? Of course, I shall!
For the beauty, and the eloquence
Of His whole creation,
Brings to naught relevance,
Of worthless speculation.
I surmise many a theory,
Everywhere will form,
Where dismal days and faces teary,
Life's scenes will adorn.
Yet vernal bloom of fragrant flowers,
Happy will sing.
As near approaches the day and hour,
Presence of the King.
Ephemeral is thy gloom,
Eternal life He brings!
It was for something…not for nothing,
And surely not a dream!

02-25-2015

The following writing done by Tristan is titled "Introduction To Esoteric Poetry."

Introduction to Esoteric Poetry

Philosophy exalts life, leading us to examine the reasons we have arrived here—here being the earth—and why we are alive! Physically, materially promotes death in that it fogs and desensitizes the delicate faculties of the human soul, which should embrace and respond to the powerful impulses of spiritual creative thought.

Hence, I stand on philosophy, dance and teach through poetry, and live eternal to the

Lord. I struggle, I am a man. I have my sins, but I war against my flesh, just as the Word of God declares through the apostle Paul, "I have to discipline my body on a daily basis in order not to be disobedient to the Gospel of our Lord and Savior, Jesus Christ."

We must engage, enter into the battle, do what we're called to do—all for the glory of our great God and Savior.

Now, look, see, and behold, I touch the very heart of all who read and understand my poetry, "Esoteric Poetry." For those who don't know what *esoteric* means, I'll do my best to explain. It means knowledge given only to specially initiated. One must already possess a certain degree of special knowledge to understand me. If you don't, yet you can understand me, then you have been initiated…in spirit!

Esoteric Poetry

Take note, I won't be modest, there exist none to compare,
    Read the words which dance-romantic,
        Rhyming, hanging in the air.
In the Temple, did I pass through, long ago, initiation,
    Sow the scripture in the Prophet's heart,
        Till the time of revelation.
To the world, I came a sinner, criminal, with reddened eyes,
    And God has chosen this foolish man,
        Now, to confound the wise.
    Now believe or stay in doubt,
    But I'm now employed by the Lord.

    Raise my head from sad defeat,
        And be knighted,
        With His sword.

ROBERT HERNANDEZ

All the rest of my life's days,
I'll fulfill my purpose swiftly,
You may call me Tristan Ray,
And I am sent to uplift thee.

02-25-2015

This next writing by Tristan is titled "Play with No Title."

Play with No Title

Intriguing dream most lucid spins the weaver,
Upon the astral light.
Unfamiliar plants and trees, with breeze doth dance,
And silent sing.
Floating...I a heavy fog, an ephemeral misty bliss,
Through the mystic landscape, I,
Am by the tree leaves kissed.
Celestial music takes the form of scents,
And scents are sounds.
And sights are sounds,
And round and round,
Vision profound,
Hath Ariel enchanted me? Or Gabriel thus charmed?
Or Raphael or Michael bent the light,
This Dream rests on?
Through the fabric...astral...quilt,
Resting where visions are built,
Interfaced so brilliantly, obscured from the profane.
Stands the matrix of high dreams.
Touch what can't be heard or seen,
Again, shall we... The play go see,
Never to know its name!

A spark from the divine flame!
08-04-2015

This next writing by Tristan is unfortunately for me the last writing of Tristan's that I have, even though it's not done according to dates. It's titled "Skyward Ascension."

Skyward Ascension

Skyward ascension,
surround me with love.
Escorted by Angels to heaven above,
I'm awe-stricken…Dumb!
Cannot utter a word,
Hearing a language I've never heard,
I'm blind…yet I see,
For not with my eyes,
My mind failing me, foolish to surmise,
For flesh, I have not,
As I first look down,
No body, no ground, bright light all around.
Who is this now coming in my direction?
You seem familiar to me, though unseen,
Study I strongly with great circumspection,
Where did I meet thee? In maybe a dream?
(God speaks)
My son, I have watched thee,
In all of your days,
I am in knowledge of all your ways.
Away now with doubt, fear, and circumspection!
I am the life,
And the resurrection.
(I speak)
Truly, my Lord, You know all that I've done,
And I am ashamed to look You in the face,
(Gabriel the Angel speaks)
Such it is child, here with everyone,
Behold the mystery, of this, His grace.

02-25-2015

Tristan wrote that this writing of his was to be in two parts, but unfortunately, I, the author, have been unable to find the other part. I apologize for this.

The following commentary is my personal relationship that I had the privilege of spending with Tristan the last six months of his precious life.

So how does one begin to explain how one has been blessed with one of God's greatest gifts? The love of another human being—a pure love, one that simply loves for the joy of loving?

Before I go into my meeting with Tristan, I'd like to share a little about myself so you may have some idea of how I came to know and love this precious child named Tristan Ray Thompson. I've been a practicing follower of Jesus Christ for the past twenty-two years. I've spent most of my adult life in prison, and it was on my way back to prison for an infraction I was not guilty of where I met Tristan.

Upon my arrival at the federal prison where I met Tristan, I first met a child by the name of Richard, who had just given his life to the Lord Jesus Christ. And I had heard from the other brothers on the yard that just prior to Richard giving his life to the Lord, he would go around and literally beat up the followers of the Lord verbally, and now, he was proclaiming to serve the living God. For most of the brothers who endured his abuse, it was hard for them to accept. Sort of the biblical account of the apostle Paul, when he gave his life to the service of the Lord. Not many of the then brothers in Christ believed him, but time will prove all things.

So this precious child, Richard, went about asking some of the brothers on the yard who knew the Word of God, and I can only assume one of the brothers in Christ gave him my name. On the day I met Richard, he had such a hunger and thirst for the Word of God that it delighted me. I remember asking him the following question—what would you like to know about the Word? And he replied everything. Great attitude! I would that all who seek to know the living God had this very same attitude. Anyway, now, I'll get to the part where I first met Tristan.

One day while I was walking to the kitchen, Richard came up to me and said, "Hey, brother, there's this guy out on the recreation field that I walk the yard with every day, and every day, he asks me questions about the Word of God. And I don't know the word that well. Would you be willing to talk to him?"

And I said, "Sure, I'll talk to him." And so the following day is the day I met Tristan Ray Thompson.

Richard and I were walking out to the yard the following morning, and as you enter the recreation yard, there is a shack where you could borrow sports equipment. And there, next to the shack stood Tristan. As I drew closer, I observed he was a "white man," shaved head, tattoos all over his face, and I thought to myself, *Oh boy, what did I get myself into this time, Lord?* This was my introduction to Tristan.

What a joy he was and still is in my journey through life. I was honored and privileged to know this precious child. From the first moment he spoke, I perceived this was a very intelligent child. Once the introductions were done with, Tristan began by stating he was told by Richard that I knew the Word of God very well, and I replied that I know a little about our Lord's Word, and if he asked me a question and I didn't have an answer for him at the time, I would go back to my room and research the word for the answer and that I would do my best to bring it to him the following morning. I also told him I would not engage in a debate over the Word of God. If he asked a question, I would answer him with the Word of God, and if he didn't like the answer, to take it up with the Lord.

He was a little taken aback by this response of mine, stating that his experiences when it came to discussing the Bible, almost everyone desires to prove that what they're saying or desiring to teach is the very Word of God. I replied that God Himself doesn't feel the need to defend His word and He certainly doesn't need my help to defend His word. God's Word stands by and of Himself, whether I believe it or not. If anyone needs to defend their stand concerning God's Word, it's the person themselves they need to look at, and not God. God's Word is perfect, just as God Himself is.

So this is how my relationship with Tristan began. As I've said earlier, from the very first question that Tristan asked me concerning the Bible, I knew this was a very intelligent and gifted young man. I fell in love with the preciousness of this child from that very moment. So from that time on, I would meet with Tristan and Richard every morning for an hour of Bible questions. This lasted approximately three months, and then, I was sent to another yard for my last six weeks. After I had been there three weeks, lo and behold, the prison guards brought someone to my cell to be my roommate, and who should it be—Tristan.

So needless to say, the remaining three weeks I had left to do, Tristan and I stayed up, constantly talking about the Word of God and all the things he wanted us to do when he was released. For even though he was from Kentucky, after the passing of his dad, his mom moved to Tucson, Arizona, exactly where I lived. So he had all kinds of ideas that he desired to accomplish upon his release.

To say that my time with this precious, gifted child was not only unique, but also, it had turned out to be one of the greatest blessings I've ever received from the Lord God. And in saying that, I would say that that is an understatement. It was as if we had known each other all our lives; we just enjoyed each other. We enjoyed our time together. Wouldn't it be great if we as people would just be grateful and enjoy the precious gifts of God that He brings into our lives, those precious human beings that come into our lives, and make our lives so much richer for knowing them? As for Tristan and I, it's as if we were, and had always been, the very best of friends, and that's exactly the relationship we had.

Tristan became to me the very best of a friend one could have here on the earth. I'd like to go back a bit here to share with you, the reader, to what I consider a very high honor in the prison system. It's when one inmate offers another inmate personal access to family members. This is something that isn't done very much in a prison environment.

Anyway, when Tristan and I first met, I didn't know this at the time, but Tristan was calling his mom, Angie, and telling her all about me. Anyway, one day, Tristan says to me, "Hey, you need to call my mom. She's waiting for your call." And he gave me her phone number.

I remember telling Tristan, "Your mom's not waiting by her phone for me to call. Everybody out there in the free world has cell phones."

And Tristan tells me, "Just call. She's waiting to hear from you!"
So this is how I came to know Tristan's mom.

When I reflect back on all the things that were going on to bring this precious child into my life, I am overwhelmed with the awesomeness of the Almighty God. As I stated earlier, about six weeks before my release, I was sent to another prison complex, never getting the opportunity to say goodbye to anyone. So I had no idea what Tristan must have thought. But as I said, three weeks later, here comes Tristan to the same place, and then ends up as my cellmate. Incredible!

What makes this even more incredible is the fact that in prison you're separated into ethnic groups, and I was Hispanic and Tristan was White. So the guards had to ask me if I was willing to take a white man for a cellmate, so I had to get up from the bed and go to the door to see this person. And lo and behold, it's Tristan. The smiles on both are faces could have lit up a major city. The joy of seeing each other was overwhelming. As I said earlier, to love and enjoy another human being, for the pure joy of just being able to share your love unconditionally with them, is heaven on Earth.

Upon my release, when I returned to Tucson, I would occasionally call Tristan's mom to see how Tristan was doing. And we entered into a friendship, that as time went by, became more secure. What I didn't know at the time was God had some very different ideas than what I had. As you'll see from this following statement, Angie became my wife, and all I know is that this also was a miracle from God.

To begin with, as I've said earlier, I've been raised Hispanic all my life, and one huge tradition we as Hispanics have is to not marry outside our own race—or I should say, this was a huge part of my life. Anyway, needless to say, the Lord wiped away sixty years of racial indifference in a moment, and I fell in love with this precious child called Angie. And now, I have a wonderful life, and it's in part because I have a wonderful wife. And all this came into existence because of the Almighty God, who, in His awesome wisdom, allowed me to meet Tristan.

The following experiences I will share with you the reader is about the last five months of Tristan's life as well as I can remember it. For the most part, Tristan, his mom, and I spent most of our time together during these precious last months of Tristan's life.

The first time I saw Tristan was the day of his release from the halfway house he was in. His mom told me the following story about that day. She had picked Tristan up from the house he was at and was taking him shopping for some things, but she first wanted to stop by and see a friend for a few minutes. She said that Tristan kept asking her who it was she wanted him to meet, and she would keep putting him off. And I was walking home from the store and had just crossed the street onto the street in I lived on when Tristan and his mom came around the corner. Wow!

The joy we both had upon recognizing each other, it was like we were both kids, and we were dancing in the street. What a joyous and blessed time was that first meeting of ours.

We ended up going to my house and spent some quality time, just visiting each other. Tristan was so happy to see me, to know I was there for him, as I said I would be. This was in March 2016, and we spent some of the most wonderful times together, until his going home to be with the Lord, on August 14, 2016.

From that time on, Tristan, his mom Angie, and I spent as much time together as we possibly could. Even though Tristan and his mom lived about thirty miles from my house, they would come over two to three times a day. Tristan was so excited about being out, all he would ever talk about is all the things he desired to do. He had such great aspirations, great goals he desired to accomplish. He was so full of zeal for life.

I also got to see another side, or I should say, I got to see many other sides to Tristan I never knew about. For one, every time we would be in his mom's car and we'd pass a homeless person, Tristan would always ask his mom to stop and give the person some help. I learned about his compassionate heart for those in need. But at the same time, I saw his struggle to be accepted by a society he had been rejected.

We spent time together every day after that. It was such a wonderful time. One day, Tristan invited me to come spend some time out at his mom's house, and we ended up going to the pool and just spent time playing like little kids. All the time, he kept trying to entice his mom to get into the pool with us, but to no avail. Anyway, that night, both Tristan and I stayed up most of the night, talking mostly about all the things Tristan wanted to accomplish now that he was out. I remember spending the night there, me lying on the floor and Tristan on the couch, just enjoying our time together, and the next morning, enjoying breakfast before I left to go home.

Yet later that day, here comes Tristan and his mom over to visit me once again. It was just a wonderful time to spend with such a wonderful child. Even though Tristan went through some difficult times during these five months, his struggle with his weaknesses, he still desired to do the right thing. And from most of his efforts, he did his best. But I have to say this, his best wasn't good enough; so in the end, he gave it all back to the Lord Jesus Christ. And that is how this writing came to be called "the Miracle of Tristan Ray Thompson," for I've personally saw the miracle in Tristan's life. How, in the end, when he gave himself over to abstaining from the use of all illegal drugs and alcohol, went on the medication prescribed for him, I knew that our Lord had brought him back from his backslidden state.

Tristan had two incidents while he was out, both were behind his drinking and his drug use at the time. It would break my heart to see him when he was under the influence of these substances, but it would just bless me with an opportunity to pray for him. I believe that if most people who truly understood the struggles this precious child has gone through in his life, I believe that most would be sympathetic toward this child's struggles. It truly amazes me how this precious child became the gifted and talented child that he was. That in itself would be considered a miracle; his whole life is a reflection of the great love this child had for others, regardless of how he himself had been treated by family and society.

So because of these two incidents, Tristan came to live with me in my house for the next three weeks. I had one of life's greatest adventures, and some of the most interesting and peculiar experiences with Tristan. I remember the first day he came, he was so excited to be staying at my house, but at the same time, he was trying so hard to be respectful of my home. By this, I mean that both my brother and

I were followers of the Lord Jesus Christ and that we desired for him to follow certain rules, which he agreed to do. But it was a challenge for my brother when Tristan would fall back into sin. At those times, I would tell my brother Jesus loves him "just as much as he does you, so why don't you just pray for him."

I'd like to go back to the first day Tristan came to my house and the reason he was there. He'd just had his second incident that involved the police, and upon his release from the county jail, which is over thirty miles from my home, he somehow found his way to my house. I heard the doorbell ring, and when I went to answer the door, there stood Tristan, about twenty-five away from the door.

And I heard him say, "I didn't even know if you wanted me to come to your home."

I was so filled with joy just to see him. I told him, "Get your ugly self in here." And that's how Tristan and I ended up spending the next three weeks in my house.

What an adventure living with this precious child was. As I've said before, the best way to describe Tristan was that he was a "living tornado"! So for the next three weeks, Tristan and I spent almost all of our time together. His mom would come over and visit almost every day. We would go out to eat, or I would make breakfast for Tristan and his mom, Angie

I remember getting Tristan settled into the spare bedroom we had in our home. And during that first day, he behaved himself just like a little angel, but in the morning, Tristan had taken over my living room, turning it into his bedroom. He just seemed to take over the whole house. It seemed as if this was just a part of his nature, to take charge as if he was in charge. He was an awesome child.

He had this habit of coming into my bedroom throughout the night, two or three times a night, always with a cup of coffee, and always with this question, "Are you awake?"

I would always respond, "I am now!"

So he'd come in and begin a conversation with me about whatever was on his mind. Sometimes it would be about what he desired to accomplish with his life—to be a healer and a teacher, to lead young men and women to come to now the one true God. He would talk about all the things he wanted to do with his mom and myself. He was just so filled with life. It's a sad loss that this world, for the most part, will never have the opportunity to know this precious and gifted child.

Every morning that he lived at my house, he would come into my room about 4:15, and say, "Hey, old man, you up? Let's go outside and watch the sun come up. I made us a pot of coffee."

So we would both go out back on the porch and talk and watch the sun rise up every morning. We did this every day for the whole time he spent at my house. After the sun was up, we go back inside, and Tristan would always offer to make us breakfast, and not just for the both of us, but also for my brother. Not only would he cook, but he would always clean up afterward.

Tristan fought a very hard battle with his drug and alcohol use. He so desired to be set free, but in his own strength, he was unable to overcome his demons. And even though I would forgive him when he would fall, it still broke my heart to see his struggle. And if there was one thing Tristan came to know about me and my relationship with him is this, that I loved him regardless of his weaknesses. He came to know that in his heart.

At this time in my life, I was in the hobby of restoring furniture, and Tristan was excited to want to lend a hand. And I remember his mom telling him, "Now, Tris, you wait until Beto tells you what to do before you start to help."

But Tristan, bless his heart, had such a great desire to help me, he would get up earlier than I would and go out and begin to work on the furniture. Before I realized what had transpired, Tristan had destroyed three pieces of furniture. When I saw his work, I remember telling him, "Good job, Tristan. Let's go inside and take a break."

His mom and I would just laugh over his big heart and his efforts to help. He so blessed my life.

Throughout all this time I was spending with Tristan and his mom, I began to see a love between mother and child that I have to admit I've never seen before. Tristan's mom, Angie, was Tristan's best friend, his greatest fan, and his place of refuge here upon the earth when family and society had rejected him. This love that Tristan and his mom shared is one of the greatest loves I've seen between a son and his mother. The world would be a much better place if all sons and daughters would love their mothers as much as Tristan had loved his mom. I've got some of Tristan's poems written just for his mom, and I'll share these later.

After three weeks, Tristan decided he had to be with his mom, so he moved back with her about the end of July. At this time in Tristan's life, he was under a lot of stress due to the two incidents he had been involved in. So I came to understand how he needed to be with his mom. And he so desired to be through with his drug and alcohol problems.

Finally, his mom found a program, and he began his medication. And from my own personal experiences with knowing hundreds, if not thousands, of people who have gotten on a methadone program to quit their drug use, I've never encountered a single person who quit the use of all illegal drugs and alcohol. Period. To me, this was a miracle in and of itself. Here, this precious child did something that thousands of others have failed at, even though they've all said that they've wanted to quit and were unable to.

This begins the last week of Tristan's life here on the earth. From the first day he went on the methadone, he abstained from every illegal drug, and he stayed away from all alcohol. He was truly happy, if that is the proper word. His mom said he was the happiest she had seen him since his father passed away in 2012. And I can also say that this time in Tristan's life was the happiest I'd seen him since the first few times I saw him when he was released from the halfway house.

Anyway, that last week of his life here, we would go out to eat. We just enjoyed the peace that had come into Tristan's life. He was no longer troubled by his demons that last week. He was filled with the love, joy, and peace that can only come from God. I remember the last night Tristan lived here, his mom had gotten tickets to a place called the Desert Museum, and she had called me to ask if I wanted to go with them. And I was sick that evening, and I was unable to go.

But later that evening, Angie called me from the Desert Museum and told me Tris was running around the museum like he was a little kid. Angie said he was so full of joy. He had with him a friend that he would call his Queen Dee, and he was pulling her around like a little kid. I remember thinking to myself, *He's in such a good place. Thank you, Lord, for bringing this precious child back and delivering him from his demons.*

The next time I heard from Angie, his mom, was early in the morning August 14, 2016, telling me Tristan had passed away. So I told her I was on my way. As I've said earlier, that at the time, we lived about forty-five minutes apart from each other. When I arrived at her house, I was led into the room where Tristan lay, and I knew he had passed on. I laid my hands on him, prayed Psalms 23 over him, and I cried.

As I've said earlier, I believe Tristan was taken into the presence of our Lord and Savior Jesus Christ when he fell asleep. And here's my reason for saying this, that last night of his life, when he and his mom were coming home from the Desert Museum, Angie, his mom, told me the following story.

That during the ride home, they were listening to a radio station called K-Love. A song was playing that had the words, "There is power," and Tristan had laid his head on his mom's shoulder and told her how much he truly loved her. Then he began to sing the song on the radio at the top of his voice. "There is power." He even went so far as to lean out the passenger window and sing the song at the top of his voice to the world. And when he was done, he once again laid his head upon his mom's shoulder.

There's a scripture that has the following words in it, "If you don't become as a little child, you will in no way, enter into the Kingdom of God." Tristan showed the little child he was during that last week of his life. He came to trust in God with his whole heart. God himself calls us to come back from our backslidden state, and I saw the miracle in Tristan's life as our Heavenly Father called his son back home, back into the family, where he will always be accepted, always be loved, never to be rejected again.

This is a sad truth in our lives of today, that many of our children today are rejected by many in society, by parents, by peers, by almost all those in authority. So where do our children turn to? The streets, drugs, and alcohol, or acceptance through sexual encounters.

Why can't we just love the precious gifts the Lord God blesses us with? Why can't we encourage those that have endured great struggle? Why do we feel we have to belittle others who have made mistakes, who have weaknesses just as we all do? I believe we lost this precious child, Tristan Ray Thompson, simply because those that should have given love to this child withheld the love that was needed to help this child to become the great child he was meant to be.

Even though I attribute this to family, friends, and those in authority that came into his life, I ultimately know it was the enemy of mankind, Satan. But just as the enemy thought that his greatest victory over Jesus Christ was the cross, so it is with Tristan. The enemy might have believed that if he took Tristan's life he would have victory over Tristan, but as with the Lord, he made a big mistake. I know where this precious child now exists—in the very heart of the one true God.

All the writings of Tristan's that I've written, I didn't know they existed until after his passing. As I've said, I found out so much more about Tristan after his passing than I ever did while I shared the last six months of his life with him.

In conclusion, I'd like to say the following: Tristan was one of my life's greatest blessings. I shall always be grateful for the preciousness of this precious gift I had the honor to know and love. I shall always treasure the precious memories of Tristan. As I've said earlier, he had the ability to touch hearts with his love and compassion for others, and he certainly touched mine.

THE MIRACLE OF TRISTAN RAY THOMPSON

ROBERT HERNANDEZ

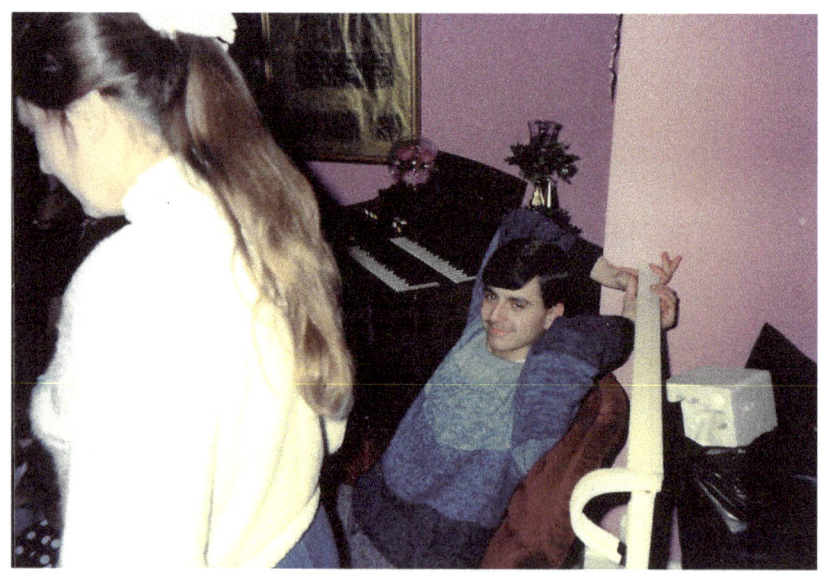

THE MIRACLE OF TRISTAN RAY THOMPSON

About the Author

I am a follower of Jesus Christ and have been serving the Lord for twenty-three years. My desire is to touch hearts for the Kingdom and Glory of God.

CPSIA information can be obtained
at www.ICGtesting.com
Printed in the USA
BVHW022142160621
609642BV00013B/2566